Investing in Hedge Funds

Investing in Hedge Funds

A Guide to Measuring Risk and Return Characteristics

Turan G. Bali

Yigit Atilgan

K. Ozgur Demirtas

AMSTERDAM • BOSTON • HEIDELBERG • LONDON
NEW YORK • OXFORD • PARIS • SAN DIEGO
SAN FRANCISCO • SINGAPORE • SYDNEY • TOKYO
Academic Press is an imprint of Elsevier

Academic Press is an imprint of Elsevier
The Boulevard, Langford Lane, Kidlington, Oxford, OX5 1GB, UK
225 Wyman Street, Waltham, MA 02451, USA

First published 2013

British Library Cataloguing-in-Publication Data
A catalogue record for this book is available from the British Library

Library of Congress Cataloging-in-Publication Data
A catalog record for this book is available from the Library of Congress

ISBN: 978-0-12-404731-0

For information on all Academic Press publications
visit our website at **store.elsevier.com**

This book has been manufactured using Print On Demand technology. Each copy is produced
to order and is limited to black ink. The online version of this book will show color figures
where appropriate.

Working together
to grow libraries in
developing countries

www.elsevier.com • www.bookaid.org

CONTENTS

Participants in financial markets are not a homogeneous group. Different investors have a unique set of risk and return expectations that have changed significantly over the past few decades. The asset management industry has managed to increase its size exponentially due to its ability to satisfy these expectations. Consequently, there have always existed a set of alternative investments that are designed to service those investors who do not want to settle for the risk and return combinations that traditional investments offer but prefer to experiment with novel asset classes. The composition of this alternative set of investments has also evolved remarkably through time. Several decades ago high-yield bonds, emerging market equities, and real estate were considered to be alternative. Today, such investments would rather be classified as traditional. The current alternative investments are private equity, venture capital, precious metals, commodities, and even art works. One of the most important items on this list is hedge funds.

Hedge funds are considered to be alternative investments because their returns are deemed to be uncorrelated with those of traditional asset classes and the risks underlying hedge fund investments are unique. Although the hedge fund industry has grown tremendously in the recent past, there is no simple definition of what a hedge fund is. Moreover, the public has not reached a consensus regarding whether hedge funds have merits in terms of expanding the investment opportunity sets of investors or they serve to destabilize the financial markets due to the opportunistic actions of fund managers. Hedge funds have been considered as sophisticated asset classes that operate in a deregulated environment and viewed as approachable only by high net-worth individuals. However, these alternative investment vehicles are quickly getting more transparent, regulated, and institutionalized. In other words, there are many misconceptions that need to be clarified about hedge funds.

One of the objectives of this book is to present a brief review of the hedge fund world. We recognize the heterogeneity among hedge funds but also identify some common features that hedge funds share such as investment flexibility, low transparency, illiquidity, an expensive fee structure and active management. We discuss the pros and cons of investing in hedge funds and underline some new trends in the industry after taking a historical perspective. We compile a condensed review of the academic work on hedge funds. We also provide a taxonomy of hedge fund strategies and summarize the rationale behind each strategy.

The main goal of the book is to provide a comprehensive investigation of how hedge fund indices have performed over the last 20 years. There are two dimensions of the performance of any financial asset, namely its risk and return. One cannot make sense of one attribute without having knowledge about the other. Therefore, most of the book is devoted to present risk and return characteristics for a wide range of hedge fund indices. Different from earlier studies, we examine different measures of risk and calculate alternative reward-to-risk ratios for each index. Some of the risk measures we construct are particularly appealing for hedge fund indices as they take how much value a hedge fund index can lose with respect to a previous high or as a result of an extreme event. We compare the reward-to-risk ratios across hedge fund indices as well as tracking the ratios over time. In the process, we explain hedge fund data biases and index construction methodologies as well as the differences between investable and non-investable hedge fund indices. Finally, we analyze the determinants of hedge fund index returns such as the higher-order moments of return distributions and the exposures of index returns toward various macro-economic and financial factors.

We emphasize that none of the material presented in this book is intended for use as an investment advice. Our goal is to shed some light on the world of hedge funds by implementing a detailed risk and return analysis based on the historical data. Investors must always keep in mind that the history is not a perfect indicator of the future in financial markets. Moreover, even if one is confident in an investment strategy, the execution of the strategy requires expertise. We hope that the readers keep these points in mind while absorbing the material in this book.

Introduction

1.1 WHAT ARE HEDGE FUNDS?

It is not an easy task to come up with a precise and succinct definition for the term "hedge fund." The hedge fund world is an ever-changing one, and this is a major reason why there is no exact and universally accepted legal definition for hedge funds. One can say that they are private pools of capital in the sense that ownership claims in a hedge fund are not traded in organized exchanges, and fund investors benefit from appreciations in the market value of a hedge fund's asset portfolio. It is well known that hedge funds present investment opportunities which provide risk and return combinations that are different from traditional equity and fixed income investments. Other than these, hedge funds vary significantly among themselves in terms of investment strategy, risk, and return characteristics. Some hedge funds are large, and others are small, measured by the assets they have under management. Some hedge funds are on the way to becoming household names, whereas others choose to operate discretely. Technological innovations have revolutionized the hedge fund industry and contributed to the heterogeneity that had been already inherent in the business. What cannot be denied is that hedge funds now constitute an alternative financial system by themselves. They act as the primary liquidity providers for relatively more obscure assets such as distressed debt, replace traditional financial intermediaries as lenders to speculative grade corporations, and function as insurers of last resort for risks that used to be hard to manage. Also, hedge funds have become the primary investors in listed companies raising equity privately. Brophy et al. (2009) report that companies financed by hedge funds are generally poorly performing firms with substantial information asymmetries. Companies that raise capital from hedge funds underperform companies that raise capital from other sources, implying that hedge funds act as equity providers for firms that cannot otherwise access equity financing.

Although there is a lot of heterogeneity in the hedge fund industry, it is possible to list some common traits that most hedge funds share. One of these traits is the flexibility that hedge funds enjoy. Indeed, this flexibility is the main factor that differentiates hedge funds from more traditional investment vehicles such as mutual funds. The performance of mutual funds is measured with respect to a benchmark, and any deviation from the benchmark is considered as risk. So, for the traditional asset management industry, risk is assessed on a relative basis. When market benchmarks are plunging in value, it is natural to expect that mutual fund returns will also go down with these benchmarks. This is not valid for hedge funds since hedge funds claim to focus on absolute returns, and, consequently, risk is also assessed in an absolute sense. What hedge funds care about is not the direction in which the overall market is moving, but the ability to spot relative price discrepancies between multiple securities and exploit these opportunities.

Hedge funds can achieve this absolute return focus thanks to their expanded toolbox compared to that of mutual funds. Hedge funds do not face regulatory restrictions regarding the financial instruments they are allowed to trade or their portfolio compositions. Unlike traditional investment vehicles, hedge funds can use derivative instruments such as options and futures, and they are able to bet on price declines by short selling securities. Chen (2011) reports that 71% of hedge funds trade derivatives, and derivatives users exhibit lower fund risks and are less likely to liquidate under poor market conditions. Although the practice of short selling has often been criticized by regulators and corporate executives who face public and investor pressure when firm values decline, short selling is instrumental for helping asset prices to revert back to their fundamental values for overvalued securities, and hence it enhances allocational efficiency in the economy. Moreover, short selling is not a costless strategy and should be used very carefully by hedge funds when they take short exposure. The risks associated with short selling will be discussed in Chapter 2 when we describe hedge fund strategies that focus on this practice. When used with caution, short selling may help hedge funds maintain an absolute return focus and generate positive returns independent of the direction of the movements in the general markets.

Another dimension of flexibility enjoyed by hedge funds is their ability to borrow money to magnify their returns. This practice is called "leverage." The notion of leverage is a double-edged sword and increases the risks faced by hedge funds since leverage magnifies not only gains, but also potential losses. For example, if the fund portfolio is constructed by borrowing 90% of total asset value, the portfolio could become worthless after just a 10% drop in the markets. Finally, hedge funds have fewer obligations compared to mutual funds regarding their capital adequacies. All this flexibility has its benefits and costs. It is true that hedge funds can adapt to market conditions easily compared to other investment vehicles; however, they are also subject to more manager risk since a hedge fund manager has a lot of discretion over how the fund is run.

Another common feature of hedge funds is that the regulatory and tax framework surrounding them is not stringent. Many hedge funds are registered in offshore tax havens around the world, and there is not much transparency regarding their operations. The Securities Exchange Commission (SEC) passed an act in December 2004 that requires certain hedge funds to register with the SEC; however, this act was struck down by the Federal Courts in June 2006. Brown et al. (2008) investigate the hedge fund disclosures beginning with the first filing date in February 2006 and find that these disclosures contained useful information regarding the funds' operational risks. This information is undoubtedly important for hedge fund investors. However, for hedge funds, transparency is an undesired attribute because funds that take strategic positions or short sell particular securities would not want their trades to be known by outsiders. Supporting this hypothesis, after new disclosure rules were passed in 2010, Agarwal et al. (2013) focused on the holdings of hedge funds that were requested to be confidential and found that these confidential holdings were associated with more information-sensitive stocks and produced higher abnormal returns compared to the nonconfidential holdings. On the other hand, fraud risk becomes substantial in a lightly regulated industry since investors are unable to monitor the hedge funds using conventional methods, and they do not even know in which type of assets their money is invested in. The lack of transparency has enabled some hedge fund managers to cook their numbers and lie to the public about their performance. Even if the investors are suspicious about fraud, they cannot just take their money and leave the crime scene due to restrictions for redeeming capital in the hedge fund business.

This brings us to the issue of illiquidity. Hedge funds are not liquid investments. To start with, even the wealthiest institutions and individuals need to wait for specific dates or time windows before they can subscribe to hedge funds, since most funds do not let investors in on an ongoing basis. More importantly, investors cannot redeem their invested capital from the hedge funds whenever they desire. There are lock-up periods which correspond to minimum amounts of time that an investor is required to keep his or her money invested in a hedge fund before the investor is allowed to withdraw capital. These lock-up periods are especially pronounced at the initial phase of a hedge fund and may prohibit investors from redeeming their money for up to a few years. Even when the investors are allowed to redeem their money, there are certain conditions that need to be satisfied. Redemption periods are often set at the end of fiscal quarters, but they can even be less frequent. Moreover, an advance notice up to three months should be given to the hedge fund before the redemption. Funds may also have special provisions called gates that limit the amount of capital that can be withdrawn at each redemption period, or funds may charge extra fees for redemptions. These fees often decrease in amount as the capital is kept in the fund for a longer period to incentivize investors not to withdraw their money.

The rationale behind the illiquidity of hedge fund investments is that these provisions enable hedge fund managers to invest freely in illiquid assets. Illiquid assets may turn out to be very profitable investments, but they may require a long-horizon focus because it may take time before the profits can be realized. Many valuable investment opportunities in financial markets are not compatible with the idea that hedge funds should maintain continuous liquidity for their clients. In a liquid world, hedge funds would have had to maintain cash reserves as liquidity buffers, and since cash generally earns lower expected returns compared to riskier investments, this would hurt a hedge fund's overall performance. Another drawback of liquidity is related to the adverse impact of early withdrawers on existing fund investors because potential asset sales could spur additional transaction costs that would be borne by existing clients.

The expensive fee structure underlying hedge funds is also a common feature. Hedge funds charge their clients an annual operating fee, typically about 2% of assets under management just like mutual funds, but on top of this, hedge funds also impose additional performance or incentive fees that are generally about 20% of fund returns. This "2 plus 20" formula is common in the industry, and it is possible to encounter performance fees that are even higher and reach half the gains generated by the hedge fund. This type of fee structure may not always justify the returns generated by fund managers even if the gross returns are higher than the ones generated by traditional money management vehicles. The situation is even worse for funds since these entities invest in different hedge funds themselves and then charge additional fees to the investors. The rationale behind this fee structure is that hedge funds try to attract the brightest minds and the best talent to their businesses by compensating their managers based heavily on their success. The drawback is that this type of reward system is asymmetric, and fund managers receive a portion of the profits, but they do not share the portfolio losses. As a result, hedge fund managers may take too many risks in their investment decisions. One way to mitigate the problem of undue risks is obligating the fund managers to invest their own money in the fund.

A protection against extravagant fund fees is the high watermark system that means that hedge fund managers can charge performance fees only after the hedge fund surpasses its historical peak. In other words, past losses must be recovered first before fund managers earn the right to incentive fees. Of course, any protective system will come with its own drawbacks, and the notion of high watermarks is no exception. Employees of hedge funds that are far away from their high watermarks may opt to go and work for other hedge funds that are performing well. Worse, such funds may choose to close shop and reconstitute themselves. The problem regarding managerial incentives to take too many risks is still relevant since the objective to reach high watermarks may push fund managers even further to gamble and hope that their bets pay off. There are two possible variations on the high watermark system. First, there exist proportional adjustment clauses that allow managers to reduce the amount of loss to be recovered in order to receive incentive fees with proportion to the amount of money that investors withdraw from the hedge fund. Second, there are clawback clauses which require a certain portion of incentive fees to be deposited in an independent account so that the clients can be partially compensated if the future fund performance turns out to be poor.

The academic literature has also shown interest in the impact of managerial incentives in hedge fund behavior. However, the evidence so far has been mixed. Kouwenberg and Ziemba (2007) analyze the relationship between incentives and risk taking. They find that incentive fees reduce a fund manager's level of loss aversion and, hence, can result in increased risk taking. A mitigating factor can be the manager's own stake in the fund, which may curb the propensity to pursue risky strategies. Agarwal et al. (2009b) measure the extent of managerial incentives by the sensitivity of option-like incentive fee contracts to changes in the fund value, levels of managerial ownership in the fund, and the existence of high watermark provisions. Their results suggest that such incentives are positively associated with higher risk and superior fund performance. Hodder and Jackwerth (2007) occupy a middle ground and argue that the impact of incentive contracts on risk taking is dependent on a fund manager's employment outlook. For fund managers who are close to their contract termination or who are facing a probable fund closure due to poor results, incentive-based compensation contracts cause fund portfolios to be tilted toward riskier strategies.

On the other hand, if the fund manager still has several evaluation periods in the future, then the risk-taking behavior is much more restrained regardless of the incentive system. There are also studies in the literature that find no evidence between incentive contracts and risk taking. Brown et al. (2001) cannot find any proof that fund managers engage in more risk taking to take advantage of incentive contracts, and indicate that a manager's behavior is instead driven by the performance of peer funds. The strong linkage between performance volatility and fund termination tames risk taking, and fund termination is closely linked with the industry benchmarks even after the distance to high watermark thresholds is accounted for. Similarly, Aragon and Nanda (2012) find that managers whose incentive pays are linked to their fund's high watermarks are less likely to increase risk. The authors argue that the popularity of high watermarks in the hedge fund industry may be driven by the demand of investors who favor the role of these instruments in tempering the managers' behaviors. Also, the study argues that shutting down and restarting a hedge fund due to high watermarks or resetting these thresholds is costly in terms of both the legal expenses and the reputational costs.

Hedge funds are in the business of chasing after arbitrage opportunities. In today's financial markets in which arbitrage opportunities are short-lived and fleeting, the notion of buy-and-hold is incompatible with the nature of hedge funds. Therefore, portfolio turnover is very high for many hedge funds, and trading costs such as bid-ask spreads, commissions paid to the brokers, and stock-borrowing costs can amount to about 5% of portfolio value on average.

Mutual funds can be passively or actively managed, but hedge fund managers are active by definition. The performance of hedge funds can be either beta or alpha driven. When we say beta driven, we mean that a hedge fund that exposes itself to some market or macroeconomic risk will naturally get compensated for that risk. For hedge funds, on top of traditional sources of beta such as equity market and bond market performance, there are also alternative sources of alpha such as liquidity, volatility, corporate event risk, and commodity market performance. Alpha represents the abnormal returns earned by hedge funds that cannot be explained by risk exposures. In the hedge fund business, alpha comes from either the regulatory flexibility awarded to hedge funds or the fund manager's ability to pick the right securities to invest in at the right times. The competitive advantage of hedge funds comes from the ability to collect and analyze information more efficiently, the valuable human resources that possess special insights, the low cost access to financial markets, and superior trade execution.

Given all the advantages and disadvantages of hedge funds, the industry has grown immensely in the past. According to Hedge Fund Research, a leading hedge fund data provider, the industry had $39 billion of assets in 1990 whereas the assets under management had reached $2.375 trillion in the first quarter of 2013. This is up fourfold since 2000 and up almost twofold since the beginning of 2009, a time period before which the hedge fund industry lost a lot of assets due to the global financial crisis. During the first quarter of 2013, there was a flow of $15.2 billion of net new capital to the industry of which $9.4 billion was from fixed income-based relative value strategies, and

$3 billion was from global macro strategies. In 1990, there were about 600 hedge funds, and this number increased to about 10,000 in 2007. Although many hedge funds were forced to close down during the credit crunch of 2008, the number of active hedge funds has now returned to its peak. Even with this rapid growth, the hedge fund industry makes up only 4–5% of the assets in global financial markets. However, hedge funds are responsible for a disproportionate amount of trading volume. Estimates suggest that hedge funds drive 25% of trading in organized exchanges, and this percentage is much higher for more obscure financial instruments such as distressed debt and leveraged loans.

Despite this growth trend, there may be a natural limit to the size of the hedge fund industry. After all, there are diseconomies of scale in the hedge fund business. Many hedge funds specialize in small niches of the financial markets and constantly plow these niches to generate returns. However, arbitrage opportunities are not endless in the financial markets and, as more money gets poured into the industry, the hunt for mispriced securities is going to get more competitive. There is a limit to how much cash individual trades can absorb, and any extra cash is going to get invested in second-rate bets that fund managers would have skipped over in the past. Going forward, it will not be easy to find low-risk arbitrage opportunities, and this may be one of the reasons why hedge fund returns have been going down in the last decade. As a consequence, many of the most successful hedge funds choose to close their doors to new investors due to fears of return dilution.

Many investors prefer to park their money in hedge funds because they believe that they are delegating the management of their savings to truly skilled professionals. Modern financial markets present many complex opportunities to talented players to realize returns. Hedge funds are able to bet on the changes in the relative pricing of multiple securities or even whether a movie is going to be successful in the box office or not. Hedge funds have the required resources such as human capital and computer power to exploit these opportunities, and this is why they have the potential to generate absolute returns. A side benefit of the nature of the hedge fund business is that the complex strategies result in return profiles that have low correlations with traditional financial instruments. This is important because low correlation implies more diversification benefits and the enhancement of risk-return profiles for investor portfolios.

Another benefit of hedge funds is that they provide liquidity in the markets, especially for riskier companies, so that it is easier for businesses to raise money with a lower cost of capital.

Aside from their benefits, hedge funds also get a lot of criticism from trade unions and industry protectionists. Hedge funds are perceived by some as aggressive capitalists that are only interested in short-term profits. It is argued that hedge funds make too much money at the expense of ordinary investors, and the fact that they are lightly regulated brings up issues of fraud and leaves scope for market abuse. As such, hedge funds are the usual suspects and scapegoats in periods of financial crisis. During the credit crunch in 2008 and 2009, the voices of parties who attack the hedge fund industry got louder. Regulators pointed out that a hedge fund that was selling short a corporation's shares and at the same time buying protection against default via credit default swaps could undermine market confidence and accelerate market meltdowns. Moreover, as witnessed during the credit crunch, when the crisis finally materializes, hedge fund investors could ask for their money back subject to redemption restrictions, and the ensuing security sales by the hedge fund industry could make asset prices fall even faster than they would have normally.

Another problem is herding between hedge funds. If many hedge funds have similar positions and exposures, they may experience losses in tandem with highly damaging liquidity and volatility consequences. Herding is especially problematic if hedge funds move to illiquid asset classes such as mortgage-backed securities simultaneously. When this happens, artificial liquidity improvements and price hikes occur, causing illiquid securities to seem less risky than they actually are. When the reality sinks in, and the funds realize that their positions were not so liquid after all, existing risk management techniques may prove inadequate, and large scale financial contagion may occur. Boyson et al. (2010) document evidence of worst-return contagion across hedge fund styles for the period between 1990 and 2008 and identify liquidity shocks as a fundamental driver of this contagion.

1.2 THE HISTORY AND THE FUTURE

The creation of the first for-profit hedge fund is commonly credited to Alfred Winslow Jones in 1949. However, as explained by L'Habitant

(2006), on whom we will base our brief historical account, there were earlier indicators of hedge fund activity. Karl Karsten was a statistician who published a book about scientific forecasting in 1931. Karsten's interest in finance did not come from his desire to make money, but from the fact that financial markets proved to be a fertile ground to test his statistical theories. He had "barometers" such as trade volume, building activity, interest rates, industry indices, and wholesale price levels to forecast the business cycles. At the end of 1930, Karsten set up a small fund to exploit these barometers, and during the first six months of its existence, the fund was able to refrain from losses while making gains that became permanent. Moreover, this performance profile was independent from the general movements in the stock markets. Karsten also wrote about some basic fund strategies that are still used today (albeit in a more complex manner). He advocated an investment strategy based on purchasing stocks that are anticipated to increase in value the most and short selling stocks that are anticipated to decrease in value the most compared to other stocks. This is the foundation on which the technique of statistical arbitrage, which will be described in Chapter 2, is based.

The first for-profit hedge fund set up by Alfred Winslow Jones is a precursor to the equity hedge strategies that are commonly used today. Jones believed that he was a good stock picker in the sense that he could identify stocks that would beat the market and stocks whose performance would fall short of the market. He also believed that he could time these price movements accurately. As a result, he took long positions in undervalued stocks and short positions in overvalued stocks. This way he was also able to minimize the exposure of his fund to movements in the overall markets. Jones was also using the proceeds he got from his short positions to finance his long positions, and the resulting leverage served to magnify his returns. Short selling and leverage were not new concepts, but Jones combined these two instruments in such a way that the resulting fund portfolio was conservative in risk, but promised high returns conditional on a superior stock picking ability. This idea is still at the core of equity strategies that are used commonly today. In the 1950s and 1960s, Jones' fund performed well. During this period, Jones began not trusting solely on his stock-picking ability, and, consequently, he hired other portfolio managers who had autonomy by themselves so that the fund became a model for today's diversified multimanager hedge funds.

It was not until 1966 that Jones' fund business came under spotlight due to a newspaper article, and this was the first instance in which the term "hedge fund" was used to describe the philosophy behind the fund's investment mandate. After this, many hedge funds were created, of which many imitated the strategy of Jones' fund in the hope of replicating its performance. Due to the bull market of the 1960s, many of these new funds either took unprofitable short positions since they lacked experience in such trades, or they ignored the short side of the investment style completely to use a long (only with leverage) strategy. The bear market of 1969 and 1970 triggered huge losses which got even more pronounced in the 1973–1974 depression. During this period, many hedge funds went bankrupt, and market liquidity dried up.

In the late 1970s and early 1980s, the markets moved horizontally with some troughs and peaks. During this period, the number of active hedge funds was low, and they were generally operating in secrecy and restricted to wealthy individuals. It was another print article in 1986 regarding the supreme performance of Tiger Fund which popularized hedge funds once again. The investment strategy of this fund was much different as it did not just restrict itself to equity and ventured into financial derivatives. Also, Tiger Fund did not focus on hedging, but rather took directional bets on macroeconomic activity. This period was suitable for such macro strategies since the US dollar was weak, commodity and equity prices were going down, and bond markets were on the decline due to increases in the interest rates. During this period, many hedge funds undertook directional bets on macroeconomic indicators, but in October 1987, the markets crashed, and many hedge funds again were drastically hit. However, this time, the markets and hedge funds recovered quickly and made up for their losses. Some hedge funds even came under spotlight due to their huge successes driven by leveraged directional positions. One example is the Quantum Fund that earned about one billion dollars by betting against the British sterling in 1992.

Public concerns about hedge fund strategies were being pronounced at the start of the 1990s. When the Federal Reserve increased interest rates unexpectedly, many hedge funds had to deleverage to get out of their positions that were funded by margins, and this deleveraging caused bond prices to fall even more and reinforced the impact of the Federal Reserve's decision. The Asian and Russian crisis of 1997 and

1998 strengthened the public perception of hedge funds as shady entities. Before the 1997 Asian crisis, a speculative bubble had built in emerging markets such as South Korea, Taiwan, and Thailand due to heavy capital inflows driven by the perception that these markets had large upside potential. When the financial crisis erupted, prices in these markets declined rapidly both for real and for financial assets. Although some big-shot hedge funds also went under in these periods of market turmoil, due to the massive short positions that some macro funds took, the public came to blame hedge funds for their destabilizing actions.

The bankruptcy of Long Term Capital Management (LTCM) in the wake of the Russian financial crisis in 1998 served to enhance this perception even further. LTCM bet on its expectation that the spread between high- and low-quality bonds was going to narrow, and its positions were highly leveraged at the beginning of 1998. In August 1998, the Russian government decided to devalue its currency, default on its domestic debt, and declare a moratorium. This decision led to a panic in financial markets since many Russian financial intermediaries terminated their derivative contracts by using special clauses, and the counterparties of these contracts lost the positions that insured and hedged against their other investments. The ensuing flight to quality caused the spreads between high- and low-quality bonds to widen even more, and LTCM lost its equity capital only to be saved by a rescue from the government and other players in the financial sector. This incident made the need for more transparency and prudent practices more urgent in the hedge fund industry. Many hedge funds became more careful with their risk management practices and reduced the leverage underlying their positions.

The period after 2000 witnessed two more financial crises. The first one occurred in March 2000 when the dot-com bubble burst and the NASDAQ index plummeted. According to Brunnermeier and Nagel (2004), hedge funds did not have a correcting effect on security prices during this period because they were heavily invested in technology stocks. Hedge funds were fully aware of the bubble and they chose to ride it by capturing the upturn, but reducing their positions in stocks that were about to decline in value. Thus, although many hedge funds had long exposure toward technology stocks, the industry came out relatively unscathed from this crisis.

The second crisis occurred due to the problems in the subprime lending sector and the associated structured financial products such as mortgage-backed securities. The first warning sign came in August 2007 when BNP Paribas terminated withdrawals from hedge fund clients due to lack of liquidity, and the full blow occurred in September 2008 when several major financial institutions came under duress starting with the fall of Lehman Brothers. Although some hedge funds made a fortune during this period due to their net short exposure, most of the hedge fund industry was caught on the wrong side of the markets, and the industry faced a big contraction during this period. Ben David et al. (2012) investigated the trading behavior of hedge funds during the crisis. They found that hedge funds withdrew from the equity markets collectively in this period and their sell-offs were driven by the capital redemptions by their investors and pressures by their lenders. Furthermore, hedge funds gave priority to stocks with high volatility when they liquidated their positions, and they also sold the most liquid securities in their portfolios to constrain the price impact of fire sales. As argued by Liu and Mello (2011), these asset sales and the consequent liquidity hoarding suggests new limits to arbitrage for hedge funds since the funds were unable to activate their arbitrage capabilities in a very opportune time period. Recent industry reports suggest that the hedge fund industry is back on its feet and the size of the sector is back to its precrisis situation in terms of both assets under management and the number of active hedge funds.

In the recent past, there was a big shift in the hedge fund industry regarding its clientele base. The times in which hedge funds catered almost exclusively to high net worth individuals and family offices are over. According to a KPMG industry report issued in 2013, these two categories hold 43% of hedge fund assets, whereas pension funds and other institutional investors have a 40% stake. The remaining 17% is held by funds of hedge funds, and these entities also cater to many institutional investors. This is a big change given the fact that institutional investors have traditionally preferred to stay away from hedge funds due to their lack of transparency and high fees.

Increased involvement of institutional investors in the hedge fund business has spurred more demand for transparency, especially after the financial crisis. Now, investors want to know more about the individual positions that hedge funds take and their asset compositions.

There is also demand toward operational transparency regarding the kinds of software models and trading arrangements that hedge funds are employing. The culture of the hedge fund industry and the sector's readiness to be more open toward their investors has undergone a dramatic change in order to appeal to more businesses. After the Dodd-Frank Wall Street Reform Act passed in July 2010, funds in the United States with more than $150 million under management or 15 clients are required to register with the SEC and file information regarding their trading positions. Some hedge fund managers who are exempt from this act also chose to register with the SEC to satisfy institutional investors. Demand toward more transparency has also coincided with greater focus on due diligence and a push from regulators for new registration and reporting rules. These changes may prove to be too costly for small hedge funds. Higher legal and compliance costs and more human resource and infrastructure requirements are likely to put small hedge funds out of business.

The continued flux of institutional investors has the potential to spark a consolidation wave in the hedge fund industry as these institutions are often attracted to big names and track records. They also demand stronger corporate structures and more reliable risk management systems that can only be satisfied by funds that exceed a certain size. The evidence regarding whether larger or smaller hedge funds generate better returns is mixed. On the one hand, there are studies such as Ding et al. (2009), which argue that large funds that experience positive liquidity shocks outperform small funds that experience negative liquidity shocks on a risk-adjusted basis. On the other hand, there are studies such as Aggarwal and Jorion (2010), which document that small emerging funds exhibit superior performance during their initial years but, as they age, become more risk averse and lose their edges. Regardless of which hypothesis holds true, the consolidation of the industry will give more clout to big fund managers, and this may result in longer lock-up restrictions or taller gates. Another consequence of the institutionalization of the client base is that new investors such as pension funds and endowments are entrusted with other people's money, so they demand sustainable returns. This has the potential to impact the risk-taking behavior of hedge funds. We are facing a period in which hedge funds are likely to stop taking big risks to generate big returns, but will instead focus their energies on setting up a robust structure in their businesses.

Another trend that may impact the future of the industry is related to liquidity. The recent crisis showed that hedge funds had a severe liquidity mismatch, and many were forced to sell some of their illiquid assets at fire sale prices. Many funds set up gates that limited the ability of their investors to withdraw money, but this has caused reputational losses. In the future, it is possible that we will witness fee reductions in exchange for longer lock-up periods. The recent financial crisis has already brought some downward pressure on hedge fund fees. Fee structures may get differentiated among hedge funds based on their strategies, risks, and asset bases.

Coggan (2008) argues that the liquidity problems during the credit crunch caused some hedge fund managers to consider a practice called permanent capital. Under this practice, a portion of the investors' capital in the hedge fund cannot be redeemed. The benefit is making the financing secure and enabling the fund managers to invest in illiquid assets without worrying about redemptions. To ensure liquidity for clients, the whole hedge fund company or some specific funds could be floated and traded in the market, which is akin to imposing a closed-end structure on the hedge fund. Under this arrangement, investors would have to sell their shares in the open market rather than redeem their money directly from the fund. This would also have the advantage of giving small individual investors easy access to the hedge fund world. The downside is that, as is obvious from the example of investment trusts, shares in a closed-end fund do not always trade at net asset value. Actually, there exists a secondary market for hedge funds, named Hedgeway, on which transactions on funds that restrict inflows and outflows are executed. Existing hedge fund investors can trade their stakes with one another in this market, and Ramadorai (2012) documents that these trades occur at prices which often deviate from the end-of-month net asset values that hedge funds report. The idea of turning hedge funds into closed-end entities can also impact the incentive structures of the hedge fund managers adversely since they will not be accountable for redemptions.

In the past, the boundaries between hedge funds and mutual funds have disappeared in entities called "hedged mutual funds." These entities are mutual funds in their legal status, but they mimick hedge fund strategies. Agarwal et al. (2009a,b) find that hedged mutual funds have superior returns to traditional funds due to their flexible strategies, but inferior returns to pure hedge funds due to their more stringent regulations and weaker performance incentives. There are also managers who manage a hedge fund and a mutual fund simultaneously. Deuskar et al. (2011) suggest that these hybrid investment arrangements enable the mutual fund industry to retain its best managers by giving them the opportunity to manage a small hedge fund on the side. Chen and Chen (2009) investigate the conflicts of interest caused by the concurrent management of hedge funds and mutual funds; however, Nohel et al. (2010) find no evidence of welfare loss for investors due to the exploitation of such conflicts.

Coggan (2008) points out that the future may further bear witness to boundaries between hedge funds, private equity groups, and investment banks getting murkier. This trend is already underway. Private equity managers traditionally buy stakes in unlisted companies and hope to make returns from the illiquidity premium that these companies demand. As hedge fund managers need to find new profit opportunities, they have already ventured beyond the traditional arena of publicly traded securities and begun buying private companies or buying public companies and taking them private. Some examples from the recent past include ESL Investments' acquisition of Kmart and Cerberus' bids for Toys'R'Us and Texas Genco. The hedge funds have a competitive advantage over private equity groups since they have lower return expectations, faster access to financing thanks to their prime brokers, and lack of institutional pressure in hostile transactions. The downside for hedge funds is that they have to be relatively more liquid with respect to private equity groups, and they may lack the expertise in creating value in private companies since hedge funds have traditionally been scavengers on the hunt for value. Recently, we have also witnessed some private equity groups launching their stand-alone hedge funds.

A similar story can be told for investment banks and hedge funds. On the one hand, the investment banks act as prime brokers for hedge funds, contribute investment ideas, provide financing, amass seed capital, and offer start-up advice and marketing services. They may even provide office space and technological infrastructure for hedge funds. On the other hand, the investment banks' proprietary trading desks are in constant competition with hedge funds using the same techniques and instruments and operating in the same markets. Indeed, many hedge fund managers come from backgrounds in proprietary trading desks. Bank trading desks played a role in driving LTCM to destruction in 1998, but the hedge funds also were influential in the demise of some investment banks during the recent financial crisis via their shorting practices. It is natural to expect that investment banks and hedge funds are going to converge in the future via more acquisitions. We have seen examples of this behavior, such as J. P. Morgan taking a majority stake in Highbridge Capital in 2004. Of course, there may be ethical concerns and clashes with corporate executives as a result of such a convergence because investment banks that are also running hedge fund businesses will inevitably find themselves in situations where the profitable trading strategy is shorting the stocks of their clients. Massoud et al. (2011) document similar conflicts of interest for hedge funds that participate as lenders in the syndicated loan markets. Hedge funds can profitably sell short the equity of their borrowers around loan origination and loan amendment dates, especially when the amendment is unfavorable or the credit quality of the borrower deteriorates.

The hedge fund industry has been known for its adaptability and its ability to reinvent itself. Going forward, hedge fund managers will continue to discover new strategies, instruments, and markets where profit opportunities exist. It is also important to note that as time passes, hedge funds are becoming more mainstream rather than acting like the black holes of the financial system. A quick glance at the history of financial markets makes it obvious that what is defined as alternative has changed immensely over the years. Once upon a time, domestic stocks and bonds were deemed to be alternative. Investors considered real estate and emerging market stocks to be alternative in the 1980s. Today, these assets are typically in the portfolios of well-diversified investors. Surely, the definition of the term alternative investment will continue to change, and hedge funds will no longer be alternative investments in the future.

1.3 ACADEMIC PERSPECTIVE

Fung and Hsieh (1997) are among the first to investigate hedge fund and mutual fund returns in an integrated framework. Mutual funds are investments with relative return targets, and studies that assess the performance of mutual funds generally focus on the "location" component of returns, which relates to the asset categories that the mutual funds hold in their portfolios. Hedge funds have an absolute return focus; therefore, prior models that are used to explain mutual fund returns may be inadequate to explain hedge fund returns. Motivated by this, Fung and Hsieh (1997) also look at the "strategy" component of returns, which has to do with what lies under the managers' investment rationales, and the "quantity" component of returns, which has to do with the amount of leverage used. These additional components that are added to the traditional performance attribution models are able to explain returns generated by dynamic trading strategies that hedge funds use. The authors also document that returns of hedge funds have low correlations to those of mutual funds and propose additional style factors based on fund strategy.

In a follow-up study, Fung and Hsieh (2001) only focus on commodity trading advisors (CTAs), which is another term used for hedge funds that engage in managed futures strategies. These funds are directional trend followers by nature and place their bets on the momentum in asset prices. The authors set up portfolios of options called lookback straddles written on currencies, commodities, and bonds, and find that these straddles can replicate key features of trend-following strategies and explain CTA returns better than standard asset indices. The works of Fung and Hsieh have been instrumental in developing state-of-the-art performance benchmark models for hedge funds. Mitchell and Pulvino (2001) document nonlinear option-like payoffs for risk arbitrage funds and Agarwal and Naik (2004) extend these results and show that such payoffs are an integral feature of a wide range of hedge fund strategies. Agarwal and Naik (2004) also argue that many equity-oriented hedge funds have strategies that exhibit payoffs similar to those of a put option written on the market index and, therefore, are exposed to significant left-tail risk. We will revisit the notion of tail risk in Chapter 4 when we talk about how to quantify the risk underlying hedge fund returns.

Are hedge funds really superior performers? This question has been asked and investigated many times in the hedge funds literature. Although most of the studies document one form of superiority for hedge funds, there has been no shortage of studies which argue that hedge funds do not generate positive abnormal returns. Motivated by the advantages of hedge funds such as incentive alignment and investment flexibility, Ackermann et al. (1999) find that average hedge fund Sharpe ratios are higher compared to those of mutual funds despite the fact that hedge funds carry more risk. The authors link these superior returns to the organizational structures of hedge funds and show that incentive fees are significant determinants of risk-adjusted hedge fund returns. Kosowski et al. (2007) find that superior hedge fund performance cannot be explained by pure luck since hedge fund performance persists at annual horizons. Jagannathan et al. (2010) also find evidence of persistence in the performance of hedge funds. Most of this persistence is driven by top performers rather than bottom performers, enforcing the idea that managerial talent lies at the root of these findings. In their performance analysis, Fung et al. (2008) rely on data for funds of hedge funds since they believe that this data is a more accurate representation of returns earned by hedge fund investors and is less affected by data biases which will be explained in Chapter 3. They find that although the average fund of hedge funds delivers alpha only in a certain sample period, there is a subset of funds of hedge funds that consistently generates alpha.

The market timing ability of hedge funds is documented in Chen and Liang (2007), and this ability is especially pronounced in poor and volatile market conditions. Another set of evidence for managerial ability is revealed by Aragon and Martin (2012), who analyze the annual disclosures of derivatives holdings made by a subset of hedge funds. Hedge fund managers who take nondirectional positions via straddles and protective puts have volatility timing ability as evidenced by volatility increases for the underlying equities after such positions are built. Similarly, directional positions taken via plain vanilla call and put options reflect significant stock picking skills on the part of hedge fund managers since stocks in which hedge funds take call option positions significantly outperform stocks in which hedge funds take put option positions. Finally, Sun et al. (2012) investigate whether hedge fund managers who pursue unique investment strategies generate superior performance. In their study, the distinctiveness of a hedge fund's investment strategy is a decreasing function of the correlation of the fund's returns with the average returns of the hedge funds in the same strategy category. The authors find that the distinctiveness of a hedge fund is a strongly persistent characteristic and a robust predictor of better future performance.

There are also studies that question the finding that hedge funds exhibit performance superiority. Amin and Kat (2003) calculate generalized versions of Sharpe ratios and find that hedge funds are inefficient investments. These inefficiencies can be diversified by investing in funds of hedge funds, but these entities are also inefficient due to their more expensive fees. According to the authors, the main benefits of hedge funds materialize only when they are used as components of portfolios due to their weak correlation with market indices. Griffin and Xu (2009) decompose hedge fund returns into three components based on the funds' stock picking, portfolio rotation, and style selection abilities. In terms of stock picking, there is weak evidence that hedge funds outperform mutual funds on a value-weighted basis, and this result is driven by the large holdings of hedge funds in technology stocks during the dot-com bubble. Stock picking ability disappears for other weighting schemes and after benchmarking on similar assets. Moreover, hedge funds have no competitive advantage when they move in and out of different styles. Finally, Dichev and Yu (2011) argue that actual investor returns are not only determined by the returns of the portfolios that hedge funds hold, but also determined by the timing and magnitude of inflows to and outflows from hedge funds. Their results show that dollar-weighted returns that take these dimensions into account are significantly lower than returns of corresponding buy-and-hold strategies.

Another dimension of hedge fund performance is illiquidity that is manifested by both the nature of the assets that hedge funds hold and the lock-up and share restrictions that funds impose on their investors. Aragon (2007) investigates the relationship between hedge fund returns and restrictions that limit the liquidity of fund investors. The results imply that abnormal returns of funds with lock-up periods are significantly higher than those of funds that make it easier for their investors to redeem capital. Moreover, hedge fund alphas documented by the prior literature can be explained by such liquidity restrictions. These restrictions are directly related to the asset liquidity of fund portfolios. In other words, lock-up and share restrictions benefit the investors and allow them to capture an illiquidity premium. Sadka (2010) approaches the issue of liquidity from another angle and estimates the loading of each hedge fund based on the covariance of returns with an aggregate liquidity factor. Hedge funds that load significantly on liquidity risk outperform those that are not exposed to this type of risk. Moreover, this effect is independent of the return impact of lock-up and share restrictions documented in Aragon (2007). The rewards to bearing liquidity risk is large and, therefore, as shown in Teo (2011), hedge funds often take on more liquidity risk than optimal given their redemption terms. On a subset of hedge funds that have minimal redemption restrictions, those funds that expose themselves to more liquidity risk significantly outperform those funds who invest more conservatively. Schaub and Schmid (2013) tackle similar questions; however, they treat the periods before and after the recent global financial crisis separately. Their results indicate that the illiquidity premium documented in the aforementioned studies is specific to the pre-crisis period, and hedge funds were not able to manage their illiquid portfolios effectively in the postcrisis period, resulting in lower abnormal returns for less liquid funds.

Two other studies investigate more obscure dimensions of hedge fund performance. First, Teo (2009) focuses on the geography of hedge funds. The findings of this study indicate that hedge funds that have a head or research office in their investment region outperform distant funds significantly. These results are especially pronounced for emerging market funds and funds with less liquid portfolios. On the other hand, distant funds are able to raise more capital and charge higher fees from their clients, indicating a counterintuitive trade-off between hedge fund performance and easier access to funding. Second, Li et al. (2011) investigate the relationship between manager characteristics and hedge fund performance. Their results indicate that managers who graduate from higher SAT universities are able to generate better returns with taking fewer risks. Also, more established managers take less risk and the corresponding rewards are lower.

Studies that analyze hedge fund performance have to rely on hedge fund return data. Consequently, there is a strand of literature that focuses on the distortions in these returns. Bollen and Pool (2008) interpret serial correlation in hedge fund returns as a measure of return smoothing because if gains are reported timely, but losses are reported after a delay, returns that are independently distributed in reality will exhibit serial correlation. The authors find that the probability of serial correlation is related to the volatility and magnitude of cash flows from investors. This result provides a linkage between capital flight risk and return smoothing. Moreover, serial correlation is shown to be a robust predictor of hedge fund fraud. Bollen and Pool (2009) extend this finding and document discontinuity at zero as a substantial feature of the time series distribution of hedge fund returns. In other words, the frequency of small gains is much larger than that of small losses in the data. Moreover, this pattern is nonexistent for funds that are approaching an audit or that are investing in liquid securities. In other words, hedge fund managers distort their performance results when they have the discretion to do so and they are not likely to be monitored. Finally, Bollen and Pool (2012) identify performance flags based on suspicious return patterns. These flags include measures of low correlation between hedge fund returns and returns to style factors and various data quality indicators on top of the aforementioned serial correlation in hedge fund returns and discontinuity at zero. The results indicate that these performance flags are encountered more frequently in funds that are subsequently accused with performance misrepresentations and asset overvaluations.

Rather than relying on the anomalous properties of hedge fund returns, Cassar and Gerakos (2011) directly investigate the mechanisms through which the investment positions of hedge funds are priced and returns are reported to investors. They find that funds that rely on less verifiable pricing sources and managers who have more discretion in valuing their investment positions are more likely to report returns that are consistent with intentional smoothing. Finally, Agarwal et al. (2011) find that hedge fund returns are higher during December, which is consistent with fee-motivated return distortions at the end of each calendar year, and this result is more pronounced for managers whose compensations are more related to their performance and who have more discretion to misappropriate performance results.

1.4 THE AIM OF THE BOOK

In this book, our goal is to provide a detailed account of how various hedge fund indices have performed in the past. The data for hedge fund indices are compiled from two leading data providers, which are Dow Jones Credit Suisse and Hedge Fund Research. These databases report the performance of numerous hedge fund indices which are grouped according to their underlying strategies. Consequently, in Chapter 2, we define these strategies as well as describing the fund of hedge funds and composite hedge fund indices, whose performances are measured based on the returns of individual hedge funds that follow varying strategies. We are also interested in presenting information about the methods that the data providers employ to construct the hedge fund indices and any potential biases that may impact the data. We differentiate between noninvestable and investable hedge fund indices as we analyze index performance because noninvestable indices may reflect the returns of hedge funds that are closed to investors and the more recently introduced investable indices can provide a better picture of returns that hedge fund investors can actually realize. These methodological concerns are explained in Chapter 3. Our analysis regarding the distributional properties of hedge fund indices is also presented in this chapter. Chapter 4 presents and compares the risk-adjusted performances of various hedge fund indices. To do so, the concept of risk should be defined first because there are different dimensions of risk and it is important to construct different risk measures which account for such nuances. The comparison of risk-adjusted performances of hedge fund indices is carried out both across strategies and within strategies by focusing on substrategies. We also compare how investable and noninvestable hedge fund indices fare against each other. Finally, we analyze how hedge fund performance has changed over the years with a special focus on the recent global financial crisis. Chapter 5 concludes the book by analyzing the linkages between higher order moments of hedge fund return distributions, macroeconomic factors, and hedge fund index returns.

CHAPTER 2

Hedge Fund Strategies

The term "hedge fund" cannot be described by referring to a representative hedge fund since a representative hedge fund does not exist. A statement which argues that hedge funds are taking a certain action is likely to be misleading, because for every action that a particular hedge fund takes, there is most probably another hedge fund that is taking an opposite action on the other side of the trade. Therefore, reaching general conclusions about hedge fund strategies is difficult. Some funds take a lot of risk and make directional bets, whereas other funds manage their risks obsessively and keep their portfolios immune from market movements. Some hedge funds deal with complex financial instruments such as credit derivatives, whereas other funds just suffice with buying and selling equity shares.

Given all this variety in the hedge fund universe, there is no unanimously agreed upon categorization that describes the hedge fund industry, and each data provider has their own classification system. One of the data providers that we rely on for the subsequent analysis, Dow Jones Credit Suisse, distinguishes between 10 different hedge fund strategies. These are event driven, equity hedge, equity market neutral, dedicated short bias, convertible arbitrage, fixed income arbitrage, global macro, emerging markets, managed futures, and multistrategy. In our discussion, we will follow the classification devised by Hedge Fund Research, our second data provider, to group hedge fund strategies. Hedge Fund Research presents returns for a larger number of strategy indices compared to Dow Jones Credit Suisse and divides the hedge fund universe into four main strategy categories. These categories are event driven, equity hedge, relative value, and global macro. *Event-driven* funds exploit arbitrage opportunities that are presented by extraordinary corporate events, *equity hedge* funds seek to generate profits through stock picking and taking long (short) positions on undervalued (overvalued) equities, *relative value* funds aim to capitalize on the price imbalances between related securities, and *global macro* funds take directional positions based on their analysis of macroeconomic events. There is also a residual category of hedge fund strategies that includes emerging markets and managed futures.

The strategies that we discuss in this chapter are by no means an exhaustive list of all possible hedge fund strategies. There are hedge funds that engage in closed-end funds arbitrage and specialize on capturing the deviations between the net asset values of closed-end funds and the market price of the shares owned in these entities. Cross-listed securities are attractive for some hedge funds, and these funds can profit from situations under which the price of a cross-listed security deviates from the price of a security that trades in the home market and provides a claim to the same stream of income. There are hedge funds that bet on natural events using novel financial instruments called cat bonds whose payments are contingent upon the occurrence of a catastrophe. Some hedge funds use weather derivatives that have certain payoffs under extreme weather conditions. Even film financing or the careers of professional sports players can provide profit opportunities for hedge funds. As a general rule, the more illiquid and obscure the asset is, the likelier is the arbitrage opportunity. This is due to the fact that these are exactly the type of situations under which price distortions are likely to occur, and fund expertise pays off. Finally, it is important to remember that hedge funds constitute the frontier of innovation for the financial services industry, and hedge fund strategies are constantly under evolution. In the following summary, we aim to give a brief overview of the most common hedge fund strategies. For the strategy descriptions, we refer to our data providers as well as Stefanini (2006).

2.1 EVENT-DRIVEN STRATEGIES

Hedge fund managers who follow **event-driven** strategies seek investment opportunities based on mispricings surrounding a wide variety of corporate events including but not limited to mergers, acquisitions, spin-offs, restructurings, share repurchases, tender offers, hostile take-over bids, asset sales or purchases, legal disputes, financial distress, bankruptcies, and liquidations. Analysts need to carry out detailed bottom-up analysis about companies, and industrial sectors to be able to anticipate and/or manage corporate events. Fund managers can generate profits if they correctly forecast the outcome and timing of corporate events. Event-driven funds can invest in combinations of equity and fixed income instruments as well as various derivatives.

Distressed securities can be defined as stocks and bonds of companies that have defaulted on their obligations and/or filed for bankruptcy or securities that trade at significant discounts to their value at issuance. The market values of distressed securities may not reflect their true values due to illiquidity-related difficulties in the pricing process, inadequate research coverage, and psychological biases of investors or constraints in the trading behavior of some investor groups. **Distressed restructuring** funds follow a special type of event-driven strategy that profits if the issuer improves its financial and/or operational outlook or exits successfully from the bankruptcy process. Such strategies require careful financial and legal analysis. Managers of funds who follow distressed restructuring strategies may get actively involved in the management of companies by being a part of creditors' committees. Jiang et al. (2012) find that hedge funds are instrumental in balancing the power relation between debtor firms and their secured creditors. Consequently, when hedge funds are active in distressed companies, there is a higher probability that the debtor will lose exclusive rights to file a reorganization plan, the CEO will be replaced, and more payoffs will be done toward junior claims. Also, as a testament to their firm-picking ability, hedge funds have been successful, on average, in choosing distressed companies on whose reorganization processes they can make a larger impact. Distressed restructuring funds generally hold a net long position on distressed securities; thus from a risk perspective, they suffer from long bias. Additional risks in holding distressed securities include liquidity risk, liquidation risk, and complications that can arise during bankruptcy proceedings. Although distressed restructuring strategies may hold equity exposure, they primarily focus on debt instruments.

Merger arbitrage or **risk arbitrage** strategies aim to profit from opportunities that arise from extraordinary corporate transactions such as mergers, acquisitions, or leveraged buyouts. In the case of an acquisition, there is generally a spread between the value offered by the acquirer and the current market value of the target as the target stocks generally trade at a discount to the acquirers' bids due to the winner's curse. In the case of a merger, there may be a spread between the actual and the theoretical exchange ratios of the merging entities. Merger arbitrage funds attempt to identify such spreads and take directional positions by trading primarily in the equity or equity-related instruments of corporations. Although most funds take their positions after the terms of the transactions are announced, it is possible that some funds try to anticipate corporate events and take their positions before the announcements. Deals underlying merger arbitrage or risk arbitrage strategies are complicated and require both an understanding of the economic motives behind the deal and a proficiency in risk management techniques. The main risk behind these strategies is that the deal may fail to close or it may close under terms that are different than those announced initially. This type of risk is called the transaction risk. There is also the calendar risk, since delays in the completion of a deal may impact the fund returns negatively. Expertise regarding the legal frameworks for these corporate events is also crucial, especially for cross-border deals.

Event-driven funds that carry out **credit arbitrage** strategies track corporate events that offer arbitrage opportunities in the market for fixed-income securities. These funds prefer to focus mainly on a company's creditworthiness and use fundamental credit analysis to anticipate events that trigger changes in the credit quality of issuers. Many credit arbitrage funds use credit default swaps or interest rate swaps to transfer credit risk and interest rate risk to other counterparties in such a way that the funds generate returns if the creditworthiness of the issuer changes in the direction expected by the fund managers. Credit arbitrage funds may expose their portfolios to sovereign and convertible bonds and even equities; however, credit arbitrage strategies primarily focus on corporate debt with fixed obligations. Another identifying feature for credit arbitrage funds is that although they take positions with respect to anticipated firm-specific credit-related events, their net exposure to the broad fixed-income market is limited.

Delays in a corporate event can cause dilutions in hedge fund returns. **Activist** strategies engage in actions that directly evoke corporate events that unlock value, rather than identify companies that anticipate events in the near future. Activist funds generally attempt to find undervalued companies whose shareholder value can be increased through managerial decisions. In order to influence a company's policies or strategic direction, activist funds acquire representation in the board of directors or credit committees of the company, obtain advisory roles to management, or initiate proxy fights. Although it is possible that activists can possess a lot of clout over executives even with a small stake in a corporation, activists often acquire large shares in underperforming companies, which may lead to portfolio concentration risk for a hedge fund. Moreover, activist funds may possess insider status in a company, and the consequent trading restrictions may cause liquidity risk for the fund. Most activist funds focus on opportunities in equity and equity-related financial instruments and differentiate themselves from other event-driven funds by holding the majority of their portfolio in activist positions.

Brav et al. (2008) investigate activist hedge funds in the United States to find that these funds are able to successfully induce positive strategic, financial, and operational changes in their targets, and they attain success in achieving their objectives most of the time. This is attested by the permanent average abnormal returns of about 7% around activism announcements. Target firms also increase their payouts and improve their operating performance after activist interventions. Klein and Zur (2009) also document favorable market reactions for target firms and high success rates for activists. Although the former study argues that activist funds are generally nonconfrontational and do not seek control, the latter study also finds evidence for cases where activists gain board representation through threatened proxy solicitations. Klein and Zur (2009) also find that activist funds have a preference for profitable targets that are experiencing cash flow agency costs. Although these studies document that the actions of activist funds are beneficial for the stockholders of target firms, Klein and Zur (2011) document negative announcement returns for outstanding bonds of target firms. Confrontational activist campaigns and the representation of activist funds in the board of directors make these negative returns even more pronounced. Klein and Zur (2011) interpret their findings as evidence for expropriation of wealth from the bondholders to the stockholders.

The term "**special situations** strategy" is sometimes used synonymously with the term "event-driven strategy" because hedge funds that focus on special situations strategies also seek for opportunities in companies that are engaged in announced or anticipated corporate catalyst events such as security issues and buybacks, acquisitions, asset sales, and spin-offs. Moreover, special situations strategies are heavily involved in corporations that are in financial and/or operational distress. However, funds that primarily pursue special situations strategies differentiate themselves by focusing more broadly on post-bankruptcy equity exposure and exit from restructuring proceedings. Also, funds that follow special situations strategies constrain themselves to a smaller universe of securities and generate returns primarily by exploiting mispricings in equities and equity-related instruments.

Managers of **multistrategy event-driven** funds construct their overall portfolios based on a combination of various event-driven substrategies. Multistrategy funds do not maintain more than half of their portfolio in a specific event-driven substrategy. Such funds benefit from having the flexibility to invest in different asset classes depending on the specific event that drives a particular strategy and being able to alter the strategy portfolio according to changes in the business cycle. Security types include credit instruments that range from the most senior to the most junior, equity, and additional derivative securities.

2.2 EQUITY HEDGE STRATEGIES

Equity hedge or long/short equity hedge strategies establish both long and short positions primarily in equity-related securities. Equity hedge funds have been active in the markets for decades, and they constitute the fastest growing segment among alternative investment strategies. Generally, funds that follow equity hedge strategies aim to set up equity portfolios that profit from the stock-picking abilities of their managers. These funds generate (lose) money when long positions appreciate (decrease) in value and short positions decrease (increase) in value. The main source of return is the performance difference between the long and the short positions, and, therefore, the equity hedge strategy is also termed the double alpha strategy (where alpha represents the risk-adjusted abnormal performance of a strategy). Additional sources of return include the interest rebate from the proceeds of the short sale used as collateral, the interest paid by the brokers on the margin deposit, and the difference in the dividend payments between the long and the short positions. Having a short position in some stocks serves both to extract value out of overpriced securities and to hedge the overall fund portfolio against systematic risk. Investment decisions are made using both quantitative and fundamental analysis, and hedge fund managers have the flexibility to shift their portfolios between stocks based on their growth, size, and industry attributes. Moreover, equity hedge strategies can vary significantly based on their exposure to the overall equity market.

The ability to use both long and short positions enables hedge funds to follow alternative investment styles and makes it possible to generate returns from the relative price movements of stocks. It is this property of equity hedge strategies that make them popular. Although the fund managers may be wrong on their security selection on an absolute basis, they can still generate money if the long positions outperform the short positions on a relative basis. Therefore, in addition to plain vanilla long and short positions, hedge fund managers can employ techniques such as *share class arbitrage* by exploiting the price deviation between the common stock, preferred stock, and saving stock of the same corporation and *pairs trading* by establishing a long/short position based on the relative value divergence between two stocks whose prices should normally move together. One risk associated with pairs trading is that there are no securities that are perfect substitutes for each other, and the technique may expose the funds to unintended risks.

An equity hedge manager can use a bottom-up approach by examining stocks singularly and deciding on the ones to be purchased and sold short or a top-down approach by examining the general economy, deciding on the geographical and industrial allocations, and finally picking the actual stocks. Some hedge fund managers also follow a stereoscopic approach by combining bottom-up and top-down approaches. The portfolio of a hedge fund that follows an equity hedge strategy can be broken down to a portfolio that passively replicates a benchmark and a long/short portfolio made up from a set of long and short active positions. However, a hedge fund manager has flexibility in that he or she does not track a relative benchmark and focuses on absolute returns. A hedge fund that follows equity hedge strategies is distinguished from a traditional mutual fund by its ability to short sell securities and use leverage to build its investment positions. Although equity hedge managers typically maintain the majority of their investments in equities (both long and short), they can also trade equity futures, equity options, and even debt securities for diversifying and hedging purposes. Disadvantages of equity strategies include higher trading costs and higher turnover rates compared to traditional buy-and-hold strategies. Moreover, restrictions on short selling imposed by some security exchanges may cause delays in strategy execution.

For **equity market neutral** strategies, the acts of purchasing and selling stocks become dependent on each other because these strategies aim to eliminate a fund's exposure to the systematic risk inherent in the overall market. In other words, the fund's return is no longer driven by the movements in the equity markets, but it is dependent purely on the stock selection ability of the fund manager instead. Market neutrality can take different forms. The most primitive form is dollar neutrality whereby the fund makes equal dollar investments in the long and the short positions. A more widely accepted definition of market neutrality is beta neutrality. Beta is a measure based on the scaled covariance between a security's return and the market return. As such, it is commonly used as a measure of systematic risk. A hedge fund manager may want to maintain a beta neutral portfolio with the aim of focusing on stock selection and not waste resources to forecast aggregate returns. Beta neutral strategies make money when long positions go up more rapidly than the value losses from the short positions in bullish markets. Conversely, when markets are bearish, these strategies make money when short positions go down more rapidly than the value losses from the long positions. Although the beta exposure of an equity market neutral portfolio to the broader market can be zero, it is possible that the net exposure toward specific sectors is different than zero. This type of sector exposure can add additional risks to fund returns. For example, an equity market neutral fund may lose money if its long positions are in an industry that depreciates in value and/or its short positions are in an industry that appreciates in value. To maintain beta neutrality not just at the aggregate level, but also at the sector level, the long and the short positions need to be balanced for each sector. Finally, there is the concept of factor neutrality, which takes additional factors beyond the market performance into account. Some of these factors can be valuation ratios, growth projections, dividend yields, price momentum, and earnings revisions. Managers who seek factor neutrality use quantitative methods to identify the relevant factors that impact the performance of their funds, measure the exposure of their funds to these factors, and choose portfolio weights such that their funds' returns are independent from these factors. It may be infeasible to make a portfolio perfectly market neutral at all times because any change in stock prices will affect the market exposure of the portfolio and continuous dynamic rebalancing will be necessary. Thus, equity market neutral strategies typically constrain their long or short market exposure to be at most 10% of portfolio values. Patton (2009) documents that, although equity market neutral funds are more market neutral compared to hedge funds that pursue other strategies, about one quarter of market neutral funds exhibit some significant nonneutrality.

Equity market neutral managers need to uncover information regarding future price movements and relationships between security returns in order to take buy and sell decisions. In this process, complicated quantitative techniques such as statistical arbitrage are used. *Statistical arbitrage* aims to capture pricing anomalies while maintaining a market-neutral position. The central idea behind statistical arbitrage is that stocks with similar characteristics should be priced in the same way, on average. Thus, statistical arbitrageurs pick factors that explain equity prices and group stocks according to these factors. Stock selection involves analyzing the directional relationship between the stock returns and the chosen factors, purchasing the stocks that are expected to overperform, and short selling the stocks that are expected to underperform. The fund portfolio is inherently factor neutral since the long and short positions are chosen simultaneously to maintain factor neutrality. The central premise of statistical arbitrage is keeping a large number of open positions, rather than focusing on the price imbalances between a small number of securities. Although each price divergence does not automatically imply a profit opportunity, statistical arbitrage attempts to identify statistically significant valuation abnormalities through the law of large numbers. Although the rationale behind statistical arbitrage is simple, its implementation is complex since many arbitrage opportunities are very short-lived, and it requires analyzing historical and real-time data using sophisticated software for back-testing and best-execution purposes.

Quantitative directional strategies use similar quantitative techniques with equity market neutral strategies, and they also attempt to exploit new information that has not been totally or accurately reflected into prevailing market prices. However, managers who follow quantitative directional strategies have no concern for maintaining portfolios that are immune from systematic risk and thus keep the choice of the long and short sides of their portfolios separate from each other. As a result, quantitative directional hedge funds maintain varying levels of net long or short equity market exposure depending on the market outlook of their managers and other factors such as business cycles and macroeconomic conditions.

Funds that follow **short-biased** or **dedicated short bias** strategies employ quantitative techniques to identify overvalued companies and take more short positions than long positions. Short sellers make profits when stock prices decline so that they can repurchase shares at a cheaper price and return them to their original owners. If, instead, the stock prices increase, the difference between the short selling price and the repurchase price is recorded as a loss. Short-biased fund managers differ from market generalists in that the aim of their analysis is identifying securities that are expected to experience price drops in the future. The central premise of dedicated short bias strategies is that most managers in the asset management industry have a tendency to focus their analysis on identifying undervalued securities and buy-and-hold opportunities. Moreover, potential conflicts of interests such as the one experienced by equity analysts in underwriter firms cause good news to be reflected in asset prices in a timelier manner compared to bad news. Consequently, profit opportunities may be relatively more abundant for short sellers. On the other hand, there are many risks that are associated with short selling. The downside risk of short positions is theoretically unlimited; short sellers are affected adversely by the long-run average positive drift in equity markets, some exchanges impose restrictions on short selling, and there is the possibility that stock lenders will ask for their shares back before the short sellers realize their gains. Moreover, identifying overvalued securities does not guarantee success since stock prices may increase even further before they revert back to their intrinsic values causing additional losses due to a short squeeze. Short-biased funds attempt to reduce the risk they undertake by holding some of their overall portfolios in offsetting long positions and employing stop-buy strategies in order to reduce their loss when market prices go up.

Short-biased funds can choose to alter the extent of their short exposure to the market depending on macroeconomic conditions; however, the distinguishing feature of short-biased funds is that these funds maintain consistent short exposure over various market cycles and generate alpha from declines in equity prices. Many short-biased managers keep their eye out for companies that have weak cash flow generating abilities but high stock prices and/or companies that have high price-to-earnings ratios compared to their growth projections. Other candidates for short selling activity are firms that are likely to be a party in a failed merger negotiation, operate in industries suffering from overcapacity and have frequent auditory and financial reporting problems.

In addition to bets on the market or specific factors, value and growth exposures of hedge funds may cause them to underperform when the equity markets are going up and/or overperform when the equity markets are going down. **Fundamental growth** and **fundamental value** strategies are similar in that they both attempt to assess the valuation of a specific group of companies and build their investment theses based on the financial statements of the companies they focus on. Fundamental growth and fundamental value strategies differ from each other based on the types of companies they include in their portfolios. Fundamental growth strategies deal with firms that are anticipated to display high earnings growth as evidenced by their high price-to-value multiples, whereas fundamental value strategies deal with companies that are deemed to be undervalued with respect to their earnings potential. To be more precise, fundamental growth strategies attempt to identify profit opportunities surrounding securities that are expected to exhibit abnormally high levels of growth in various profitability dimensions in comparison to market benchmarks. Fundamental value strategies, to the contrary, seek to exploit pricing imbalances surrounding securities that currently generate high profits or cash flows compared to their market prices. In this sense, value managers specialize in companies whose potential has not been discovered. Both fundamental growth and fundamental value strategies attempt to generate profits either in an absolute sense or relative to comparable securities or market indicators.

Some equity hedge funds specialize in specific sectors in the economy. Two strategies that follow this type of sector-oriented approach are energy/basic materials and technology/healthcare. Hedge fund managers who follow sector-oriented strategies claim to have expertise in particular sectors and attempt to generate profits by identifying pricing opportunities that may not be easily understood by market generalists.

Energy/basic materials funds focus on companies whose business model is based on the production of inputs to manufacturing processes. The performance of such funds tends to be sensitive toward supply and demand forces and commodity prices. **Technology/healthcare** funds focus on companies engaged in developing and producing technology or biotechnology. Managers who have a competitive advantage in reading through scientific breakthroughs or understand the potentials of new pharmaceuticals and treatments are able to increase the value of their fund portfolios. Although these sectors' growth is high in nature, there are also risks that are driven by short product cycles and high volatility. A potential investment basis is the merger and acquisition activity ongoing in a specific sector, and sector-oriented fund managers may be better equipped to identify and benefit from such events. Merger and acquisition activity is especially prominent in the technology and healthcare sectors. Sector-oriented funds typically hold more than half of their portfolio exposure in a primary sector over various business cycles.

Managers of **multistrategy equity hedge** funds construct their overall portfolios based on a combination of various equity hedge substrategies. Multistrategy funds do not maintain more than half of their portfolio in a specific equity hedge substrategy. The dominant investment vehicles are equity and equity derivatives. Quantitative or fundamental techniques can be used to reach investment decisions, and strategies may range from diversified to sector-specific and can vary widely depending on net long/short exposure, leverage used, and factor concentrations.

2.3 RELATIVE VALUE STRATEGIES

Relative value strategy is an umbrella term that is used for investment strategies that seek to profit from the realization of a relative valuation discrepancy in the pricing relationship between multiple securities. The security types that are used in the implementation of relative value strategies are diverse and range across equity, debt, and derivative securities. These strategies generally rely on sophisticated quantitative techniques to identify profit opportunities surrounding risk-adjusted price differentials between financial instruments. Such price differentials are more likely to exist during periods of high volatility. The main difference between relative value strategies and event-driven strategies is that the performance of the former is not dependent on the outcome and timing of corporate events.

Convertible arbitrage is one of the most popular relative value strategies. Convertible securities are debt-like instruments that carry an option to be converted into equity under prespecified terms. Since they provide a potential claim in the stock market, they are desired by many investors. From a firm's perspective, when a corporation needs outside financing, it may decide to raise additional capital by issuing convertible bonds, if the managers believe that their shares are currently undervalued and want to sell them forward at a premium. Brown et al. (2012) find that companies whose characteristics make seasoned equity offerings expensive are more likely to issue convertible bonds to hedge funds via private placements because hedge funds have the ability to act as low-cost distributors of equity exposure. Additional incentives to issue convertible securities are benefiting from potentially lower funding costs and delaying capital dilution to maintain ownership control. Historically, convertible securities often traded at lower prices compared to their fair values, and this attracted a lot of interest from the hedge fund industry, which is constantly in search for new arbitrage opportunities. The standard arbitrage strategy involves holding a long position on the convertible bond and hedging this position by short selling the underlying common stock. Not surprisingly, Brown et al. (2012) also document that more convertible securities are issued when the stock liquidity, institutional ownership structure, and conditions in the repurchase markets are more suitable for short selling equities. There are several risks associated with this strategy and these risks will be detailed ahead. Over time, the competition among funds that use convertible arbitrage strategies has intensified and pushed funds to take directional risks, carry more leveraged positions, and engage in more illiquid securities to generate profits.

Convertible bonds possess the characteristics of fixed-income securities, stocks, and options. The indenture for a convertible bond states how many shares can be obtained if a bond with a certain denomination is converted into equity and at what price the shares can be indirectly purchased via the convertible bond. These attributes are called the conversion ratio and the conversion price, respectively. The quoted price of the convertible bond and the parity, the market value of the shares into which the bond can be converted, can be observed in the financial markets. The percentage difference between the convertible price and the parity is called the conversion premium. Valuation of convertible securities is fairly complex due to the fact that these investment vehicles are subject to interest rate risk, credit risk, and equity risk simultaneously. Moreover, special features that can be attached to the fixed income portion of convertible securities, such as call or put provisions, can complicate the valuation process further.

Academics have developed various approaches to valuing convertible securities. One approach, such as the one followed by Ingersoll (1977), views convertible bonds as compound options on the firm's debt and equity, which are themselves contingent claims on the firm's assets. This approach presents a closed-form solution for valuing convertible bonds; however, it is hard to implement because of its oversimplistic view of the capital structure of corporations and the difficulty of observing the market value of a firm's total assets. Another approach views the event of default as an exogenous jump and models the probability of default over an infinitesimal time interval as a function of various state variables. Finally, there are Monte Carlo simulations that consider numerous interest rate and equity price scenarios to derive a probability distribution for convertible bond values. Although these academic approaches are theoretically more sound, practitioners take a more pragmatic approach to value convertible securities and follow the so-called component approach. This approach views the convertible bond as a bundle made up of a plain vanilla fixed rate bond and an option that captures the convertibility dimension. The bond component is valued via a discounted cash flow model, and the option component is valued using a derivative pricing formula such as the Black and Scholes (1973) model.

Viewing a convertible bond as a bundle of multiple securities makes the risks inherent in convertible arbitrage strategies more transparent. First, there is the interest rate risk associated with the bond component. Common measures used to quantify this interest rate risk are duration and convexity. Duration is defined as the percent sensitivity of a bond's price to a small change in the level of interest rates, and convexity is defined as the sensitivity of a bond's duration to shifts in the yield curve. The interest rate risk of the convertible position is commonly hedged via interest rate swaps or selling interest rate futures. Second, there is the equity risk underlying the option component. The derivatives pricing literature provides the necessary tools required to quantify various dimensions of this equity risk. The sensitivity of a convertible bond's value to the movements in the underlying share price is called the delta and is commonly measured as the change in the market price of the convertible bond with respect to a unit change in parity. The concept of delta is instrumental in managing equity risk because the standard hedging strategy for convertible arbitrage is short selling a certain number of shares, and this amount corresponds to the delta of the convertible position. Delta is a function of the underlying stock price; therefore, to keep the convertible arbitrage strategy delta hedged at all times, it is necessary to continuously rebalance the hedge fund portfolio. There are also other dimensions of equity risk such as gamma which measures the rate of change in delta with respect to changes in the underlying stock price and vega which measures a convertible security's price sensitivity with respect to changes in the volatility of the underlying stock. Convertible arbitrageurs can implement various techniques to hedge against these additional equity risks if they wish to do so. Finally, there is the credit risk of the convertible issuer. This risk is especially pronounced because many convertible issuers are speculative-grade firms with high cash flow volatility and high financial leverage. Moreover, convertible bonds are mostly subordinated issues with a low priority in the capital structure. Convertible arbitrageurs may short sell the straight bond of the issuers or use credit default swaps to hedge against credit risk, but these strategies may be difficult to implement due to low-bond market liquidity or may expose the hedge funds to unintended risks such as the call risk. More recently, asset swaps have become popular because they enable credit arbitrageurs to hold on to the option component of convertible securities and transfer the fixed income component to credit buyers in the financial markets. Additional risks associated with credit arbitrage strategies include the risk of special events such as dividend payouts, the risk of the widening of bid/ask spreads between a convertible bond and the underlying share, aforementioned risks associated with short selling, currency risk for convertible bond portfolios diversified across currencies, and special risks that may arise from specific clauses in the convertible bond indentures.

Fixed-income markets provide plentiful profit opportunities for hedge funds because of the difficulty of building accurate pricing models for many fixed-income instruments due to their complex nature and the existence of multiple relative value relationships between fixed-income securities. Moreover, fixed-income markets are generally segmented because of the distinct objectives and investment constraints of different types of institutional players, and this segmentation reveals additional arbitrage possibilities. Hedge funds that follow **fixed-income arbitrage** strategies construct their portfolios by taking corresponding long and short positions in fixed-income instruments to exploit temporary mispricings between related securities. Some fixed-income arbitrage strategies aim to stay market neutral and minimize their interest rate exposure by matching their long and short positions so that the total duration of their portfolios is close to zero. Other fixed-income arbitrage strategies control the interest rate risk of their portfolios, but their focus is maximizing fund returns rather achieving market neutrality with regard to fluctuations in interest rates. There are also other types of fixed-income arbitrage strategies that take outright directional risks in the fixed-income markets and try to anticipate movements in interest rates to generate returns. As such, the term "arbitrage" may not refer to a pure arbitrage opportunity in a technical sense, but instead refer to a long/short fixed-income portfolio that is exposed to a variety of risks. Due to the fact that the opportunities that fixed-income arbitrageurs detect are usually short-lived and small in magnitude, these hedge funds depend on sophisticated quantitative valuation models and use large amounts of leverage to magnify returns.

There are many different substrategies that fixed-income arbitrageurs can use. Our aim is not to give a comprehensive list of these substrategies, but the most popular ones are going to be mentioned here. *Yield curve arbitrage* involves taking long and short positions at different points of the yield curve of the Treasury securities issued by a particular country. The yield curve gives the relationship between interest rates and bond maturities; therefore, yield curve arbitrage seeks to profit from mispricings and distortions across time along the yield curve. Short selling bonds with a shorter maturity and buying bonds with a longer maturity is called yield curve flattening, whereas short selling bonds with a longer maturity and buying bonds with a shorter maturity is called yield curve steepening. It is also possible to exploit the distortions among three maturity dates which is referred to as yield curve butterfly trade. *Long/short credit arbitrage* strategy aims to take advantage of credit-related mispricings in fixed income securities and can be implemented via credit default swaps without trading in the underlying bonds. This strategy is different than the event-driven credit arbitrage strategy in the sense that the improvement or deterioration of the creditworthiness of a company is not dependent on an idiosyncratic corporate event. *Carry trades* are positions built by going long in bonds with higher yields and financing this purchase by short selling a lower yield instrument. Since higher yields instruments are also higher risk instruments, the carry trade strategy is exposed to the risk of a plunge in value at the long side. *Capital structure* arbitrage aims to take advantage of price disparities among various securities issued by a single issuer including common and preferred equity. *Swap-spread arbitrage* is based on the spread between yields on Treasury securities and swaps and can be implemented by taking a long position in an interest rate swap and a short position in a Treasury security or vice versa depending on whether the fund managers expect the spread to widen or narrow. *Futures basis trading* seeks to exploit the arbitrage opportunities presented by the fact that the party who delivers the fixed income securities at the expiration date of a futures contract has the flexibility to choose the delivered security from a predetermined basket. Other types of fixed-income arbitrage strategies include exploiting the relative price distortions between on-the-run (latest issues) and off-the-run Treasury securities with identical characteristics and making directional bets on the TED spread which is the difference between the yields on US Treasury bills and yields on Eurodollars (certificates of deposits denominated in US dollars in non-US financial institutions) with identical maturities.

Fixed-income corporate arbitrage is a substrategy where the exploited arbitrage opportunity involves one or more corporate fixed-income instruments. This strategy commonly entails realizing a spread between multiple corporate bonds or between a corporate and a government bond. **Fixed-income sovereign arbitrage** is a substrategy where the exploited arbitrage opportunity involves one or more sovereign fixed-income instruments. Intermarket spread trading is an example of this strategy where the arbitrageur trades securities issued by different governments. Compared to other relative value strategies, the investment decisions for fixed-income sovereign arbitrage are driven primarily by global macroeconomic factors. However, sovereign funds distinguish themselves from funds that pursue global macro strategies by maintaining a lower net exposure to global fixed-income markets. **Fixed-income asset-backed arbitrage** is a substrategy where the exploited arbitrage strategy involves debt instruments backed by physical collateral such as real estate and machinery or financial obligations such as loan portfolios and credit card obligations. One example is fixed-income arbitrage on mortgage-backed securities (MBS). A typical MBS has a prepayment option; therefore, its value is uncertain, and complex proprietary valuation models are necessary to calculate the option-adjusted spread of an MBS. This spread is defined as the average spread of an MBS above the yield curve for comparable Treasury securities and measures the incremental value of the MBS with respect to the maturity-matched Treasury security after adjusting for interest rate volatility and the probability of prepayment. A fixed-income arbitrageur could exploit this spread by going long in the MBS with the highest option-adjusted spreads and hedge this position by short selling Treasury securities. It is possible to set the net portfolio exposure to interest rates to zero by choosing the MBS and the corresponding Treasury security such that the final position has zero duration.

Yield alternatives strategy is a relative value strategy, and as such, it seeks to profit from the realization of the risk-adjusted spread between multiple related financial instruments. The difference between yield alternatives and fixed-income arbitrage strategies is that the former mostly focuses on nonfixed income instruments such as common and preferred stock, derivatives, real estate investment trusts (REITs that are investment agents specializing in real estate and mortgages), and master limited partnerships (MLPs that are traded on organized exchanges and combine the tax advantages of limited partnerships with the liquidity benefits of publicly traded securities). Yield alternatives strategies are also different than equity hedge strategies in that their profits are based on the yield realized from the underlying securities rather than directional price appreciations. **Energy infrastructure** and **real estate** are substrategies of the yield alternatives strategy, and they contain more than 50% exposure to energy infrastructure typically through MLPs and real estate typically through REITs, respectively.

Volatility strategies perceive volatility as an asset class. The difference between the implied volatility of an instrument and the forecasted volatility of the underlying security may produce profit opportunities that hedge funds can exploit. Volatility strategies may be directional by maintaining exposure to the direction of the change in the implied volatility of a particular security or pure arbitrage oriented by staying neutral and isolating the pricing imbalances surrounding multiple options. Funds that expect near-term increases in the volatility of an underlying asset can typically use long straddles by buying a call and a put option with the same strike prices and expiration dates or long strangles by buying a call and a put option with the same expiration dates, but different strike prices. Selling volatility can be achieved through short straddles and short strangles. There is also a technique called iron condor that can generate profits when the implied volatility of an option is high compared to the realized volatility of the underlying asset, and it involves selling call and put options that are out of the money and purchasing call and put options that are even more out of the money.

Managers of **multistrategy relative value** funds construct their overall portfolios based on a combination of various relative value substrategies. Since these strategies rely on identifying temporary price deviations or spreads between related financial instruments, the investment thesis are generally quantitatively driven. Multistrategy funds are flexible in their security universe and can trade fixed income instruments, equity, derivative securities, MLPs, or REITs. These funds typically maintain more than 30% of their exposure in two or more distinct relative value strategies.

2.4 GLOBAL MACRO STRATEGIES

Although global macro funds accounted for a big portion of the hedge fund industry in the 1990s, their market share is much lower today. However, individual global macro funds still have larger assets under management compared to other types of hedge funds. **Global macro** strategies are difficult to characterize since they have the broadest investment mandate among the hedge fund universe. Nevertheless, there are some common features that are exhibited by all global macro funds. First, global macro funds are opportunistic and, as their name implies, their operations are global in the sense that they can invest in any market using any type of financial instrument they desire. They do not face any geographical restrictions, and they divert their resources to wherever new profit opportunities may arise. Moreover, global macro funds can hold positions in all asset classes such as equity, Treasuries, currency, and commodities and can alter their positions dynamically.

Commonly, global macro funds choose to trade in markets with high liquidity. Second, the investment thesis of global macro strategies are commonly top-down approaches and predicated on anticipating movements in macroeconomic variables such as GDP, public deficit, and balance of trade, and the impact of these movements on financial markets. When there are macroeconomic pricing imbalances, global macro funds usually set up directional positions, and their performance is dependent on the quality and timing of their market forecasts. In this sense, most global macro funds are considered hedge funds, not because they engage in hedging activity, but because they can operate in a more unrestricted way compared to traditional funds. This directional focus has caused global macro returns to be highly volatile historically, but over time, more global macro funds have begun emphasizing capital preservation and return consistency by employing risk management techniques such as stop loss rules and downside risk analysis.

Due to the nature of the strategy, funds that follow a global macro strategy can opportunistically imitate other strategies and can sometimes be perceived as multistrategy funds. In this respect, the notion of style drift is naturally built in the global macro strategy. Global macro funds are different than relative value funds in the sense that their investment success is hinged upon directional price movements in various financial instruments rather than the widening or narrowing of a valuation spread between multiple related securities. Also, global macro strategies are different than equity hedge strategies since the latter follows a bottom-up approach by focusing on corporate fundamentals.

In the case of **discretionary thematic** macro strategies, the key players are the hedge fund managers who interpret available data to forecast price movements in the global financial sectors and identify the regions, sectors, and financial institutions that present the best profit opportunities. Discretionary thematic managers may analyze vast amounts of micro-level information to build their forecasts about the macroeconomic outlook or they may focus their efforts on understanding market psychology to be able to pinpoint situations in which the market players make irrational judgments. Discretionary thematic funds can pursue momentum-, contrarian-, or volatility-based investment decisions. In contrast, **systematic diversified** macro strategies rely on little human input to make portfolio decisions. Sophisticated macroeconomic, algorithmic, and technical models are used to identify statistically robust patterns in asset returns and exploit short-lived price distortions. Although some systematic diversified funds employ counter trend models, most such funds are trend followers and aim to profit from momentum characteristics of various asset classes. Also, systematic diversified strategies typically dedicate less than 35% of their portfolio exposure to currencies or commodities over any given market cycle. Discretionary macro funds are more common than systematic macro funds. **Active trading** strategies can employ components of both discretionary and systematic strategies, and their distinguishing feature is that they capitalize on arrival of new information in liquid but volatile markets by engaging in high-frequency trading and large turnover.

Currency index and **commodity** strategies are substrategies that global macro funds can pursue, and they may include both discretionary and systematic components. The former chases profit opportunities across the currency assets class, whereas the latter is focused on opportunities across the commodity assets class. These substrategies would expect to have greater than 35% of their portfolio in dedicated currency and commodity exposure, respectively. The commodity substrategy can be refined even further into agricultural, energy, and metals. **Agricultural** strategies focus on soft commodity markets and take positions in grains and livestocks. **Energy** strategies focus on energy commodity markets and take positions in crude oil, natural gas, and other petroleum products. **Metals** strategies focus on hard commodity markets and take positions in precious metals such as gold, silver, and platinum. All of these strategies would expect to dedicate more than half of their portfolio exposure to their corresponding commodity class over any given market cycle.

Managers of **multistrategy global macro** funds construct their overall portfolios based on a combination of global macro substrategies. These strategies may either include distinct and identifiable substrategies such as equity hedge or relative value or they may blend together different substrategies in such a way that portfolio level disaggregation is not feasible. Multistrategy global macro funds can pursue both discretionary and systematic strategies, and they have a lot of flexibility regarding their geographic and asset class choices.

2.5 OTHER STRATEGIES

The growth potential of emerging markets driven by their productivity and technological improvements has historically spurred interest in the hedge fund industry. **Emerging market** strategies are attractive because they own most of the human and natural resources of the world; however, security valuations are lower compared to their developed country counterparts. It should also be noted that emerging markets are volatile, and traditional risk management techniques are sometimes inefficient. For example, diversifying a fund portfolio across emerging markets in a naive way is dangerous for several reasons. First, there is the concept of systematic contagion, which means that although two emerging markets may not seem to be linked directly by macroeconomic fundamentals, the crisis in one market may spillover to the other market due to global liquidity shocks. This means that security prices in emerging markets tend to be highly correlated in bad times, which is exactly when diversification is supposed to be beneficial. Second, many emerging markets have some flagship sectors, and holding the value-weighted index of an emerging market may not adequately diversify industry risks. Also, many securities in emerging markets are subject to infrequent trading, high transaction costs, and low speed of trade execution, and these factors may cause diversification to be infeasible. Although many emerging market securities provide high yields and returns, periods of profit making are commonly followed by periods of market meltdowns due to the fact that the extra yields and returns are just compensations for additional risk factors such as sovereign risk and fluctuations in interest rates and exchange rates. However, this volatile environment may provide opportunities for funds that believe that they can pick the right markets, sectors, and securities for investment. Funds that are categorized as emerging market funds can follow many of the aforementioned strategies such as equity hedge, relative value, global macro, or event driven based on their expertise and analysis. As such, the security universe that emerging market funds can invest in is diverse and includes equities, fixed income instruments, currencies, and commodities. Activist funds that target corporations that they deem to be undervalued or run by entrenched managers are becoming more prominent among emerging market funds. Motivated by the fact that short selling and using derivatives are restricted in many emerging markets, Eling and Faust (2010) question whether the value added by emerging market hedge funds is higher compared to traditional mutual funds active in these markets. They find that there are hedge funds that are able to generate significantly positive risk-adjusted alphas mostly due to the fact that hedge funds are more active in shifting their asset allocations and thus make good use of their flexible investment mandates.

Managed futures funds mainly invest in futures contracts, which are standardized agreements between two counterparties to buy or sell a given asset at a certain price at a certain future date. These funds are directional in the sense that they do not hedge their positions, but they are still grouped as hedge funds due to their regulatory origins and fee structures. In the early days, managed futures funds were also called commodity trading advisors because most of the futures contracts were written on commodities. Today, the futures markets are dominated by noncommodity-related futures contracts such as those written on corporate securities or currencies. Managers of managed futures funds believe that they can identify and forecast price variations in futures in the global markets; in this respect, they are similar to global macro managers. One of the differences between managed futures funds and macro funds is that the former relies more on a systematic approach based on computer models, whereas the latter relies more on a discretionary approach based on human judgment. The systematic approach relies on computer-based black box models that generate investment signals using quantitative techniques such as moving averages and trading ranges. However, the fund managers can use their discretion to rule out system signals. Managed futures managers can be purely technicians and rely solely on statistical analysis of past futures price movement or they can be purely fundamentalists and take the underlying economic and political factors into account. Some managed futures funds are momentum chasers and trend followers, whereas others are contrarian or volatility investors. The investment horizon and the types of futures traded can be different from one managed futures fund to another. It is common to see a significant amount of leverage being employed in managed futures trading.

Multistrategy hedge funds are characterized by their flexibility to invest in different hedge fund strategies depending upon the opportunities that are available to them. Multistrategy funds commonly have different trading groups that specialize on different strategies, and the chief fund manager decides on the capital to be allocated to different strategies in a dynamic manner. In this sense, multistrategy funds are similar to global macro funds, but they lack the top-down approach and the directionality of the latter. Diversifying capital across strategies has the advantage of letting the funds alter their investment approach under circumstances where certain strategies may be unprofitable. Thus, multistrategy managers aim to generate positive returns regardless of the movements in the markets and reduce the risk profile of their portfolios. A drawback of multistrategy hedge funds is that these funds may not attract the best talent due to their lack of strategic focus.

2.6 FUNDS OF HEDGE FUNDS

Funds of hedge funds are investment vehicles that allocate the money of their clients to multiple hedge funds. The main benefit for investors who invest their money in funds of hedge funds is achieving risk diversification. Each hedge fund strategy has its specific risks, and performance attributes can vary greatly between different strategies at a given market cycle. By investing in multiple funds, managers of funds of hedge funds are able to diversify out fund-specific risks. Funds of hedge funds have the choice of delegating their capital to numerous fund managers who pursue different strategies or allocate their money to numerous managers who follow the same strategy and thereby expose themselves to a certain level of strategy-specific risk. Since each hedge fund portfolio is already diversified, and monitoring a large number of hedge funds is difficult, it is important not to overreach in terms of diversifying. Other benefits of funds of hedge funds include being accessible to smaller investors due to their lower initial capital requirements and having access to closed funds due to their long-term relationships in the hedge fund world. Moreover, due to their muscle power, funds of hedge funds can request higher transparency from the funds they invest in, and this has caused many institutional investors to delegate their monitoring duties to funds of hedge funds.

There are also some disadvantages associated with investing in funds of hedge funds. In a fund of hedge funds, the clients have to pay performance fees to successful individual hedge fund managers, but if an equal number of individual hedge funds underperform, the clients will be paying performance fees for average overall returns. This can be interpreted as an implicit layer of extra fees. On top of this, there are the fees that funds of hedge funds charge their client themselves.

In this respect, the aforementioned multistrategy funds have a cost advantage over funds of hedge funds. Moreover, most funds of hedge funds are more liquid in the sense that they have shorter lock-up periods and less stringent redemption policies. Although liquidity may seem like a good attribute, it could impact investment performance negatively if the liquidity is achieved through new contributions that may cause runs on the fund in periods of underperformance or by holding some capital in cash which would generate lower returns compared to more illiquid securities that present the real profit making opportunities. If there are too many redemptions in a bearish market, funds of hedge funds may have to resort to borrowing at high costs, which will further damage the remaining investors. Funds of hedge funds could also pose some dangers to the hedge fund industry itself. Although funds of hedge funds are an important source of liquidity for financial markets, their portfolio composition decisions and position liquidations may cause forced assets sales that have the potential cascade from fund to fund. Darolles and Vaissie (2012) investigate why funds of hedge funds keep on experiencing capital outflows whereas investor interest in individual hedge funds has been backed up after the credit crunch is over. They find that funds of hedge funds are able to generate returns that compensate investors adequately after considering their double-fee structure and argue that the observed outflows cannot be attributed to the failure of funds of hedge funds to fulfill their investment mandate.

Funds of funds can be classified as conservative, diversified, market defensive, and strategic. **Conservative** funds of funds invest their capital in funds that engage in less risky strategies such as equity market neutral, fixed-income arbitrage, and convertible arbitrage, and they exhibit a lower historical volatility compared to the composite funds of funds index. **Diversified** funds of funds invest in multiple strategies across multiple funds, and their historical volatility is similar to that of the composite funds of funds index. Diversified funds tend to experience small losses in bear markets and generate large returns in bull markets. **Market-defensive** funds of funds generally invest in funds that follow short-biased strategies such as short selling and managed futures and therefore exhibit better returns during bear markets than bull markets. **Strategic** funds of funds are more active in funds that pursue opportunistic strategies such as emerging markets and equity hedge, and they exhibit a lower historical volatility compared to the composite funds of funds index.

Hedge Fund Databases, Biases, and Indices

There are several commercial hedge fund databases that compile performance data from individual hedge funds and make these data available to the investment public through subscription services. Being a part of these commercial databases is valuable for hedge funds because these databases are among the primary venues through which hedge funds make themselves visible to potential investors. Therefore, although doing so is not mandatory, many hedge funds choose to volunteer and release their performance data. The databases serve a significant role in validating the performance figures of the reporting funds. Another function the databases fulfill is constructing composite and strategy-specific hedge fund indices from the individual hedge fund data. There are many different hedge fund indices available, and, as we will see, these indices may vary significantly from each other based on several attributes. First, these databases are not representative of the entire universe of hedge funds because many hedge funds choose not to report their performance to any database or discriminate between databases. Second, among the reporting funds, different index providers cover different segments of the hedge fund universe. Third, each database uses different methods to construct its indices. Fourth, each database is exposed to various data biases which may affect the final index performances significantly. We will explain these biases ahead.

3.1 HEDGE FUND DATA BIASES

The academic literature in hedge fund research has been aware of database biases for a long time. Fung and Hsieh (2000) admit that the nature of the hedge fund industry is such that complete and accurate historical and current information on the universe of hedge funds is unobtainable. Therefore, commercial databases have their own idiosyncratic ways to cope with the incomplete information that they gather. This situation causes a number of biases in creating performance statistics. Some biases are unavoidable because they are inherently related to the life cycles of hedge funds. However, some biases are spurious, and they can be dealt with using appropriate techniques.

Unlike mutual funds whose performance data must be disclosed to the public, hedge funds may choose not to report their performances. Therefore, the hedge funds that opt to be a part of commercial databases may suffer from a *selection bias*. In other words, the reporting funds may not be a random sample of the entire universe of hedge funds and there can be material differences between funds that choose to report to databases and funds that choose to keep their performance statistics secret. For example, small hedge funds that are doing well have an additional incentive to disclose their performance data to become visible and increase the size of their business. The potential effects of the selection bias on the hedge fund performance studies are conflicting. On the one hand, only funds with favorable performance figures would want to be included in a database since the databases serve marketing purposes and a poorly performing fund would not want to advertise its inferior returns. On the other hand, there is anecdotal evidence that some managers deliberately hide their strong performance from commercial databases because they are operating at full capacity and have little to gain from further advertising their performance. Also, some hedge funds may not want to come under the spotlight to avoid the scrutiny of regulators and competitors. Finally, it may be the case that a well-performing hedge fund would want to conceal itself in order not to affect hedge fund indices positively and make its individual performance seem closer to the average. Ackermann et al. (1999) argue that these opposing forces may, at least, partially offset each other.

Most hedge fund studies rely on commercial databases but another source of hedge fund performance data is the 13F filings to the SEC. These filings are mandatory for institutional investors managing over $100 million in "equity-like" securities which can include options and convertible bonds. The advantage of these filings is that they do not suffer from the selection bias in commercial hedge fund databases. 13F filings are not commonly used in academic studies because they are only quarterly snapshots of a hedge fund's activity, and they present long-only equity positions at the advisor level, rather than the fund level. Thus, they ignore intraquarter trading, short exposure, and illiquid securities. An exception is Aiken et al. (2013) who use the information in 13F filings to construct a set of hedge fund returns that have never been reported to a commercial hedge fund database. They find that funds that report their performance to commercial databases significantly outperform funds that do not. This result is driven by differences in the left tails of the return distributions of the two groups of hedge funds. In other words, commercial hedge fund databases cannot adequately capture those hedge funds that experience large negative return shocks. Thus, studies that rely on commercial databases may overstate the average performance of the entire universe of hedge funds due to the selection bias.

Another type of data bias is the *survivorship bias*. This refers to the fact that some hedge funds are excluded from performance studies because they are no longer alive. Naturally, the historical returns reported to databases only reflect the performance of hedge funds that have managed to stay afloat meaning that the existence of performance data is conditional on the survival of hedge funds. The survivorship bias has been well documented in the mutual fund literature in studies such as Grinblatt and Titman (1989) and Brown et al. (1992). This bias is also applicable to hedge fund studies, and, in fact, the bias is even more pronounced for hedge funds because the attrition rate in the hedge fund industry is much larger compared to the mutual fund industry. Any hedge fund database contains both surviving funds and nonsurviving funds. Nonsurviving funds are funds that leave a database for reasons such as liquidation, name change, merger, and voluntary ceasing of reporting. For the last case, hedge funds that exit the database but still continue their operations are called defunct funds.

If the primary reason for leaving a database is poor performance, then the historical performance of surviving hedge funds would be higher than the average performance of the hedge fund universe. Liang (2000) compares the average performance of hedge funds that are surviving at the end of his sample period with the average performance of the entire set of funds over the same period. He finds that the magnitude of the survivorship bias is about 2% per year. The results indicate that defunct funds significantly underperform surviving funds and poor performance is the main reason behind a fund's disappearance from a database. Many hedge fund databases attempt to reduce survivorship bias by retaining the historical performance data of hedge funds that have ceased their operations. However, survivorship bias is still existent at the creation date of a database due to the nature of the information collection process. A database cannot reflect the performance of hedge funds that have gone under before the database's creation date. The funds that report to a database at its creation date are, by definition, the survivors.

The *backfill bias* is related to the possibility that, when a new fund enters into a database, the fund's returns before the inclusion date may be allowed to be back filled. In other words, the funds may enter the databases with instant histories and, consequently, this bias is also called the instant history bias. Generally, after a hedge fund is launched, there is an incubation period of a couple of years, during which the fund maintains a small size. If the hedge fund is able to post favorable performance figures during this initial period, then the fund has the option to start reporting its performance data to commercial databases for marketing purposes. It is less likely that hedge funds that do not perform well during their initial phase will show up in the databases. Therefore, there is a bias regarding how strong the backfilled performance figures are and this situation could cause average hedge fund performance statistics to be upward biased.

Other than these three major sources of data problems, there are also biases that pertain to how a database selects the funds to be included in its sample universe. Every database applies different screens to individual hedge funds before it decides to use a fund's performance data. In most cases, a database requires a hedge fund to have a minimum amount of assets under management, audited financial statements, and a certain amount of track record. The databases have relevant reasons to impose these restrictions; however, it is still the case that the performance data for a certain group of hedge funds does not get incorporated into the databases. For example, hedge funds that go under a short period after they are launched due to poor performance will never show up in a commercial database due to the restrictions regarding a fund's track record. Also, such restrictions and rules may differ between databases making it harder to compare hedge fund performance figures between data providers. Also, databases may not even agree among themselves regarding what constitutes a hedge fund. For example, some databases perceive managed futures funds as hedge funds, but others treat them as a separate category under commodity trade advisors.

3.2 HEDGE FUND DATABASES AND INDICES

Due to the fact that the hedge fund industry developed from a niche business to a substantial alternative investment class and the increasing institutional demand over time, hedge fund data has become more complete and accessible in the recent years. With this data, it was inevitable that a larger number of hedge fund indices would become available and start playing a more prominent role for investors. Hedge fund indices serve a multitude of purposes. They provide a broad idea about the performance and risks of the overall hedge fund industry and specific fund strategies. This is especially important for decisions regarding optimal portfolio composition because hedge fund indices make it easier for investors to assess which strategies are more suitable for their investment goals and how much weight hedge funds should be given in their global asset holdings. Also, hedge fund indices can act as a benchmark for individual funds and make it possible to understand which funds have superior risk and return characteristics compared to their peers.

Besides their benefits, hedge fund indices are also hard to construct. First of all, the aforementioned data biases pertaining to individual hedge funds are also relevant for hedge fund indices. Second, classifying funds into strategies is an arduous process because the strategy of an individual fund may not be clean cut and may be subject to change over time. Many indices use the styles that managers proclaim their funds to follow; however, this may be misleading and the indices may be using data from funds that should really be classified elsewhere. To be deserving of the confidence of the investment public, the rules regarding the selection of the funds to be included in an index, the weighting scheme for individual fund returns, and the mechanisms through which new funds are deleted from an index should be transparent. The index performance data should be reported timely on dates that are announced beforehand, and the historical performance data should not be amended as conditions change. There is also the question of whether a hedge fund index is investable or noninvestable. It is a widely known fact that not every hedge fund is open to new investors because some funds do not want to dilute their returns by accepting too much capital. If an index reflects the performance of hedge funds that do not accept new capital, and if these closed funds tend to be the better performers, then the index performance figures may overstate the returns that new investors can achieve by investing in hedge funds. On the other hand, including only investable funds in an index does not give an accurate picture of the performance of the overall hedge fund industry. Therefore, we will focus on both investable and noninvestable indies and clearly distinguish between them when we report descriptive statistics and risk-adjusted performance metrics.

It is possible that hedge fund indices that are focused on the same strategy but are compiled by different databases fail to move together. This may be due to different hedge fund samples under consideration, rebalancing periods, weighting schemes, and ways to cope with potential data biases. Therefore, in our empirical work, we rely on hedge fund indices that are drawn from two distinct databases.

Dow Jones Credit Suisse (DJCS) hedge fund indices were formerly known as Credit Suisse/Tremont hedge fund indices. These are asset-weighted hedge fund indices meaning that the index performance is measured by weighting each hedge fund's return with the total assets that the fund has under management. The noninvestable hedge fund indices provided by DJCS include a composite index entitled the DJCS Hedge Fund Index and 10 primary strategy categories. The strategy indices are event driven, long/short equity hedge, equity market neutral, dedicated short bias, convertible arbitrage, fixed income arbitrage, global macro, emerging markets, managed futures, and multistrategy. For noninvestable indices, three additional substrategies are also reported under the event-driven strategy. These substrategies are distressed restructuring, merger/risk arbitrage, and multistrategy event driven.

The DJCS Index construction methodology begins by defining the universe of hedge funds that the indices aim to reflect. This universe is defined as hedge funds with a minimum of $50 million in assets under management, a minimum of one-year track record and current audited financial statements. DJCS indices represent at least 85% of the assets under management in their respective strategy universe. The indices are calculated and rebalanced monthly, whereas the funds that constitute the indices are reselected on a quarterly basis. By subscribing to a rules-based constituent selection technique and disclosing the constituent funds, DJCS aims to minimize subjectivity. DJCS tracks more than 8000 individual hedge funds, and, due to the screens mentioned earlier, there are more than 900 funds in the index universe. For noninvestable hedge fund indices, hedge funds that are closed to new investment are included to provide an accurate picture of the performance of the broad hedge fund industry. Noninvestable DJCS indices are not only restricted to US hedge funds and funds from all over the world are taken into account. The data for the noninvestable DJCS hedge fund indices start from January 1994. The number of qualifying funds varies by strategy and by the quarter that the indices are rebalanced. If a fund does not report monthly performance or assets under management for two consecutive months, it is considered that the fund has failed to comply with the rules relating to the provision of financial information and is removed from the indices.

The investable hedge fund indices of DJCS are named Dow Jones Credit Suisse AllHedge Indices. These indices are designed to provide transparent, representative, and objective benchmarks of 10 style-based investment strategies of the hedge fund universe. To be included in the DJCS AllHedge strategy indices, a hedge fund should be accepting new investments and redemptions. Also, DJCS imposes some upper bounds to the minimum amount of initial and subsequent investments to a hedge fund before classifying the fund as investable. It is required that the fund is not domiciled in the United States because onshore hedge funds are typically incorporated as limited partnerships and most limited partnerships are closed structures meaning that no new investor can join in after the fund has been launched. In contrast, to borrow from the mutual fund terminology, most offshore funds are "open ended," and they allow investors to make new capital contributions on a regular basis. To be qualified as investable, a hedge fund should have no lock-up period, and it should allow investments and redemptions no less frequently than monthly. There are some strategies such as convertible arbitrage, event driven, and multistrategy that are exceptions to this rule and, for these strategies, funds that only allow quarterly redemptions are also considered to be investable. Redemption notifications are required to be given at most one month before the redemption dates, except the convertible arbitrage, event driven, and multistrategy indices, for which the notification time limit is extended to three months. The assets under management should be at least $100 million for investable funds. As is the case for noninvestable indices, funds must have a current audited financial statement and a minimum one year track record to qualify for the investable indices. An investable fund, its investment management company or any affiliate cannot be under investigation or review for reasons of wrongdoing, breach of any law, regulation, or rule.

The investable DJCS AllHedge indices are rebalanced semiannually by the following procedure. First, the open/closed status of each fund is determined. Then, the eligible funds are determined among the universe of investable funds according to the aforementioned criteria. The member funds are defined as all eligible funds whose total assets under management is equal to 70% of all assets under management in the investable universe for a particular strategy. There can be a minimum of 10 funds and a maximum of 25 funds in each strategy index. Once an eligible fund is included in an index, another eligible fund managed by the same or an affiliated fund manager cannot be included in the same index. Although the index constituents are rebalanced annually, there is also a procedure for semiannual partial balancing. DJCS began reporting investable index data in October 2004.

There are some commonalities regarding how noninvestable and investable indices are constructed by DJCS. For both types of indices, the methodology is allowed to apply fund weight caps to enhance diversification and limit concentration risk. The performance data is reported net of all fees and denominated in US dollars. Funds of hedge funds are not included in any of the indices. A fund can be dropped from the indices if it does not comply with the reporting or provision of financial information requirements. Any new funds added to the indices contribute on a "going-forward" basis only, and the historic monthly figures will not be adjusted. This serves to minimize the impact of the backfill bias. To minimize the effect of the survivorship bias, DJCS indices do not remove funds in the process of liquidation and, therefore, capture all of the potential negative performance before a fund ceases to operate.

Hedge Fund Research (HFR) also reports performance data for a variety of noninvestable and investable indices. The noninvestable indices are called HFRI indices, whereas the investable indices are called HFRX indices. HFR hedge fund indices are equally-weighted performance indices as opposed to DJCS hedge fund indices which are asset weighted. This is the main difference between the two databases. HFR justify equal weighting by arguing that this choice reduces any bias toward larger funds. HFR indices are broken down into four main strategies, which are event driven, equity hedge, relative value, and global macro.

The data for noninvestable HFRI indices mostly start from January 1990. However, there are some exceptions to this rule, and the data for some strategies start as late as January 1995. There are a total of 18 strategy indices reported under HFRI. The HFRI Fund Weighted Composite Index includes all HFRI Index constituents and accounts for over 2200 funds. HFR does not disclose the particular funds behind any index to nondatabase subscribers which is in contrast with DJCS, which makes constituent data public. Funds included in the HFRI indices are required to report monthly returns net of all fees and disclose assets under management in US dollars. Moreover, an eligible fund must have at least $50 million of assets under management and have been actively trading for at least 12 months. HFRI indices are updated three times a month in flash, mid-month, and end-month updates. The current month and the prior three months are left as estimates and they are subject to change as information comes from lagged hedge funds. All performance prior to three months earlier is locked and is no longer subject to change. Fund of funds are not included in the construction of composite or strategy indices although HFRI also reports performance data for five fund of funds indices which are explained in detail in Chapter 2. HFRI indices reflect the performance of both domestic and offshore hedge funds. When a manager lists mirrored-performance funds, only the fund with the larger asset size is included. If a fund liquidates, then the fund's performance is included in the HFRI indices as of that fund's last reported performance update. Funds are added to HFRI indices on a regular basis as HFR identifies candidates for inclusion.

The investable HFRX indices are engineered to achieve representative performance of a large universe of hedge funds. The data for investable HFRX indices mostly start from January 2005. However, there are some exceptions and the data for some strategies start as early as January 1998. There are a total of 37 strategy indices reported under HFRX. The selection of hedge funds as constituents of HFRX indices is a proprietary and quantitative process. The process includes robust classification, cluster analysis, correlation analysis, advanced optimization, and Monte Carlo simulations. Cluster and correlation analyses are performed to group managers by their true strategy categories and to eliminate outliers. Advanced optimization helps to choose weights that maximize within group correlation. Monte Carlo simulations help determine the adequate number and types of managers to replicate each strategy. The methodology behind the construction of HFRX indices defines certain qualitative characteristics such as whether the fund is open to transparent investment and whether the fund manager satisfies the due diligence requirements. HFR states that their selection methodology selects the hedge funds that, when aggregated and weighted, will have the highest statistical likelihood of producing a return series that is most representative of the reference universe of strategies. In order to be considered for inclusion in the HFRX Indices, a hedge fund must be currently open to new investment, maintain a minimum asset size of typically $50 million and meet the minimum track record requirement, which is generally 24 months. HFR screens approximately 7000 funds to identify those funds that are eligible to be included in the investable indices. The update frequency can vary, but all indices provide monthly performance statistics. Funds are typically added to HFRX indices on a quarterly basis. HFRX indices are not subject to revisions and are finalized upon the date reported. For both HFRI and HFRX indices, constituent funds are included in only one substrategy index.

HFRX data includes several investable composite indices and these differ from each other based on their scope, weighting method, or relationship with equity market benchmarks. According to HFR, these investable indices are constructed in the following manner. The HFRX Global Hedge Fund Index is designed to be representative of the overall composition of the hedge fund universe. It is comprised of all eligible hedge fund strategies. The underlying constituents and indices are asset weighted based on the distribution of assets in the hedge fund industry. The HFRX Equal Weighted Strategies Index applies an equal weight to all constituent strategy indices. The HFRX Absolute Return Index selects constituents which characteristically exhibit lower volatilities and lower correlations to standard directional benchmarks of equity market and hedge fund industry performance. The HFRX Market Directional Index selects constituents which characteristically exhibit higher volatilities and higher correlations to standard directional benchmarks of equity market and hedge fund industry performance.

3.3 HEDGE FUND INDEX RETURN DISTRIBUTIONS

The two main factors that affect investment decisions are return and risk. Each must be taken into account for understanding what has happened in the past. Of course, the future will not mimic the past; however, it is important to know about the past to conduct educated analysis about what may happen in the future. Although assessing risk and return seem to be primitive at first sight, there is no agreed upon standards to measure these two facets of investing, and this problem is even more troublesome for hedge funds. As explained in Chapter 1, hedge funds are subject to less stringent disclosure requirements than other types of managed funds. Most hedge fund managers prefer to operate secretly to avoid their competitors understanding their investment strategies and trade exposures, as this could prove disastrous for them. Until recently, regulators were reluctant to push hedge funds into more transparent disclosure practices since hedge funds were mostly private investment vehicles that catered to sophisticated and rich individuals. The increased interest of institutional investors such as pension funds and endowments is beginning to change the regulatory environment and the hedge fund industry is adjusting itself in terms of transparency in response to the institutionalization. However, the evolution is slow, and most hedge funds are still unwilling to provide detailed information regarding their portfolio positions and risks.

The return of a hedge fund is commonly measured as the percentage change in the net value of the assets that the hedge fund has under management. However, this is easier said than done. If investors are allowed to invest capital in a fund at different times during a calendar year, they would be subscribing to the fund at different net asset values. Since incentive fees are calculated as a percentage of the appreciation of the fund value, different investors would be facing different incentive fees and this situation makes it harder to calculate hedge fund returns that are net of fees. If there is no adjustment for this complexity, then investors who buy into a hedge fund in the middle of the year may have to pay full incentive fees, or they may be able to avoid incentive fees due to the existence of high watermarks although they have experienced capital appreciation. The essence of the problem is that, at the end of the measurement period, each investor will have a different appreciation or depreciation on his or her stake in the hedge fund, and the incentive fee calculations have to take this into account. Remedies to this problem include issuing a different series of shares to each investor group entering the fund at the same date or using deposits based on equalization factors to compensate investors for a potentially unfair allocation of incentive fees. Even with these adjustments, the resulting net asset values may not accurately reflect the effective performance of a hedge fund. There are other reasons why calculating net asset values for hedge funds is tricky. Hedge fund managers may act opportunistically with respect to the type of prices they use to determine asset values. There is no standard in the markets regarding how to price assets if several quotes for a particular asset are present. Also, the valuation methodologies and information sources can widely differ in the process of pricing illiquid securities for which reliable quotes are not available. All of these factors complicate the calculation of risks and returns for hedge fund indices.

This section aims to provide a detailed account of how different hedge fund strategies have fared historically. We start by presenting central tendency statistics for the sample of monthly hedge fund index returns we collect from the data providers. Access to the monthly returns requires no fee-based subscription to either DJCS or HFR. The arithmetic average return or the mean return is computed by summing each monthly return and dividing the total by the number of months. The presence of outliers can significantly affect the mean; therefore, the median is considered as an alternative measure of central tendency. When the mean and the median of a return distribution are significantly different from each other, this implies an asymmetry. As a general rule, if the left tail of an asset distribution is heavier than the right tail, then the median will be greater than the mean and vice versa.

Returns do not provide a complete picture of hedge fund performance by themselves. Two funds with similar returns may have very different performance characteristics depending on how representative the mean return is with respect to each individual fund return. This brings us to the concept of risk. As stated before, there is no consensus on the definition of risk. Risk is dependent on the nature of the investment strategy and the goals of an investor. A mutual fund manager may perceive risk as the deviation of the fund's return from that of a benchmark index, whereas a bank manager may perceive risk in terms of failing to meet capital adequacy.

The simplest measure of risk is the range which is defined as the difference between the maximum and the minimum of the return observations. The shortcoming of range is that it is very sensitive to outliers. However, the concept of range is still useful in the sense that it provides an idea about what type of extreme returns have been experienced in the past. Another tool that is useful in describing the dispersion of a return distribution is the concept of percentiles. Percentile is the value of a variable below which a certain percentage of observations fall. For example, the tenth percentile is the value below which 10% of the return observations may be found.

A more common way of measuring the risk of an investment is related to the extent of the dispersion of historical returns around their arithmetic mean. Statistically, the standard deviation of a sample of N security returns is equal to

$$\sigma = \sqrt{\frac{1}{N-1} \sum_{i=1}^{N} (R_i - \overline{R})^2} \qquad (3.1)$$

where R_i refers to each observation from the sample of historical returns and $\overline{R}$ refers to the arithmetic mean of these returns. This is also commonly denoted as the volatility of returns.

If asset returns are normally distributed, then the distributions can be characterized by their means and standard deviations only. A normal distribution is symmetric, and the frequency of observations within a certain distance around the mean is exactly known. However, returns of most financial assets have been shown to violate normality. Particularly, large swings in asset prices occur more frequently than what normality implies. This is even more pronounced for hedge fund returns since hedge funds engage in nonlinear trading strategies using derivatives and leverage. For hedge fund indices, it would not be a surprise to see substantial extreme returns as well as asymmetries around the means. We report two sample statistics, namely skewness and kurtosis, to capture deviations from normality.

Skewness is the third central moment of a return distribution and it measures a distribution's symmetry. A normal distribution is perfectly symmetric; therefore, it has zero skewness. Positive skewness implies that the asset presents a large probability of small losses and a small probability of large gains. In other words, the asset distribution has a long tail on the right-hand side, so it is right skewed. If an asset provides many small gains but is exposed to a low probability of large losses, it is said to be negatively skewed or left skewed and the return distribution has a long tail on the left-hand side. Kurtosis is the fourth central moment of a return distribution and it measures the peakedness of the distribution and the fatness of its tails. The excess kurtosis of a normal distribution is equal to zero. If a distribution has a large number of observations that lie away from the mean, the distribution is said to be leptokurtic and its excess kurtosis is positive. Conversely, if the returns are clustered around the mean, the distribution is said to be platykurtic and its excess kurtosis is negative. A leptokurtic distribution would have a distinct peak around its mean and heavy tails. For a platykurtic distribution, the tails would be thin, but the curve would have a flat top around the mean.

We have presented standard deviation as the fundamental measure of risk; however, the standard deviation has several shortcomings that may be problematic in the case of hedge fund returns. Volatility reflects the dispersion of all returns around the mean, however, doing so treats returns that exceed the mean and the returns that fall below the mean equally from a risk perspective. Philosophically, it is not obvious whether the dispersion of all returns around the mean is an intuitive risk measure from the investors' perspective. Most investors would not think of increases in their portfolio value as risk; however, the concept of volatility does not distinguish between high and low returns. Most investors have a goal in the form of an expected return or a benchmark to follow and risk is commonly perceived as falling short of such goals and benchmarks. Moreover, investors may have behavioral biases such that they may not perceive the benefits of gains equally as the damages of losses with the same magnitude. Therefore, the concept of downside risk has gained popularity both in the academic literature and in the practice. Downside risk treats returns that are lower than a benchmark as risk and classifies returns that are higher than the benchmark as opportunity. We will have more to say about downside risk when we present the risk-adjusted performances of hedge fund indices in the next chapter.

3.3.1 DJCS Hedge Fund Indices

Tables 3.1 and 3.2 present descriptive statistics for noninvestable hedge fund indices compiled by DJCS. Table 3.1 reports statistics for the full sample period beginning from January 1994, whereas Table 3.2 reports statistics for a more recent sample period which starts at October 2004. The reason why we choose to report results for this recent sample period is that the performance data for investable DJCS indices begins only at October 2004. Analyzing this recent sample period for noninvestable indices separately allows us both to comment on how the performance of noninvestable DJCS indices changed over time and also to compare the performances of the noninvestable and investable indices compiled by DJCS for the recent sample period.

Looking at the mean statistics in Table 3.1, one can clearly see that there is quite a dispersion between the average monthly performances of the noninvestable DJCS strategy indices. The best average performer is the global macro strategy with an average return of 0.975% per month and the worst average performer is the dedicated short bias strategy with an average loss of -0.228% per month. The composite DJSC Hedge Fund Index has a mean return of 0.717%. After global macro comes the distressed restructuring strategy index with an average return of 0.832%. Distressed restructuring is classified under the event-driven category in Chapter 2, and the descriptive statistics show that all event-driven strategy indices with the exception of merger/risk arbitrage have mean returns that are equal to or higher than that of the composite DJCS Hedge Fund Index. Merger/risk arbitrage index lags behind the composite index with a mean return of 0.535%. In the equity hedge category, the long/short equity hedge index outperforms the composite index with an average return of 0.769%; however, the equity market neutral and the dedicated short bias indices are among the worst performers. The convertible arbitrage and fixed income arbitrage indices that belong to the relative value category also fare behind the composite index with mean returns of 0.626% and 0.456%, respectively. The three indices that are categorized as "Other" in Chapter 2, namely, emerging markets, managed futures, and multistrategy indices, also underperform the composite index with average returns that range from 0.533% to 0.680%.

Table 3.1 Descriptive Statistics for DJCS Noninvestable Indices (Full Sample)

	Mean	SD	Min	10%	25%	Median	75%	90%	Max	Skew	Kurt	#Obs	Data Interval
Event driven	0.750	1.821	−11.770	−1.200	0.040	0.995	1.875	2.540	4.220	−2.215	13.444	224	199401−201208
Distressed restructuring	0.832	1.905	−12.450	−1.200	0.005	1.120	1.970	2.780	4.150	−2.139	13.620	224	199401−201208
Merger/risk arbitrage	0.535	1.199	−6.150	−0.770	−0.005	0.530	1.225	1.880	3.810	−0.964	7.461	224	199401−201208
Multistrategy event driven	0.714	1.970	−11.520	−1.250	−0.045	0.900	1.885	2.620	4.780	−1.732	10.368	224	199401−201208
Long/short equity hedge	0.769	2.862	−11.430	−2.310	−0.860	0.780	2.325	3.740	13.010	−0.011	6.130	224	199401−201208
Equity market neutral	0.453	2.965	−40.450	−0.520	0.110	0.680	1.275	1.840	3.660	−11.820	163.196	224	199401−201208
Dedicated short bias	−0.228	4.901	−11.280	−6.360	−3.400	−0.735	2.930	6.150	22.710	0.666	4.340	224	199401−201208
Convertible arbitrage	0.626	1.989	−12.590	−1.190	−0.030	0.965	1.490	2.160	5.810	−2.677	18.935	224	199401−201208
Fixed-income arbitrage	0.456	1.643	−14.040	−0.660	0.195	0.740	1.165	1.620	4.330	−4.439	33.740	224	199401−201208
Global macro	0.975	2.788	−11.550	−2.000	−0.180	1.050	2.145	3.520	10.600	0.018	6.824	224	199401−201208
Emerging markets	0.680	4.273	−23.030	−4.130	−1.260	1.170	2.810	5.010	16.420	−0.753	8.031	224	199401−201208
Managed futures	0.533	3.373	−9.350	−3.810	−1.860	0.345	2.945	4.940	9.950	0.025	2.945	224	199401−201208
Multistrategy	0.650	1.547	−7.350	−1.100	0.090	0.800	1.630	2.260	4.280	−1.687	8.791	222	199403−201208
DJSC Hedge Fund Index	0.717	2.172	−7.550	−1.480	−0.225	0.770	1.810	3.060	8.530	−0.181	5.434	224	199401−201208

Table 3.2 Descriptive Statistics for DJCS Noninvestable Indices (Recent Sample)

	Mean	SD	Min	10%	25%	Median	75%	90%	Max	Skew	Kurt	#Obs	Data Interval
Event driven	0.536	1.975	−5.750	−1.880	−0.260	0.850	1.800	2.800	4.220	−1.090	4.430	95	200410–201208
Distressed restructuring	0.520	1.802	−5.660	−1.700	−0.100	0.950	1.710	2.250	4.150	−1.307	5.168	95	200410–201208
Merger/risk arbitrage	0.382	1.096	−3.490	−0.920	−0.150	0.400	0.970	1.650	3.220	−0.508	4.671	95	200410–201208
Multistrategy event driven	0.561	2.204	−6.170	−2.210	−0.410	0.890	2.010	2.900	4.780	−0.949	4.252	95	200410–201208
Long/short equity hedge	0.495	2.516	−7.810	−2.290	−1.210	0.710	2.310	3.230	5.230	−0.833	3.850	95	200410–201208
Equity market neutral	−0.061	4.399	−40.450	−1.350	−0.210	0.470	1.100	1.650	3.660	−8.280	76.451	95	200410–201208
Dedicated short bias	−0.441	4.643	−11.280	−5.910	−3.520	−0.890	3.000	5.680	10.310	0.219	2.619	95	200410–201208
Convertible arbitrage	0.403	2.605	−12.590	−1.630	−0.430	0.750	1.490	2.360	5.810	−2.371	13.907	95	200410–201208
Fixed-income arbitrage	0.333	2.163	−14.040	−0.700	0.060	0.620	1.170	1.850	4.330	−3.909	24.156	95	200410–201208
Global macro	0.749	1.664	−6.630	−0.860	−0.030	0.960	1.620	2.670	4.440	−1.153	7.242	95	200410–201208
Emerging markets	0.652	3.111	−13.630	−2.840	−0.650	1.130	2.400	3.830	6.960	−1.436	7.262	95	200410–201208
Managed futures	0.507	3.191	−5.390	−4.030	−2.320	0.430	3.220	4.820	6.610	−0.042	1.864	95	200410–201208
Multistrategy	0.515	1.851	−7.350	−1.520	−0.110	0.790	1.690	2.260	4.280	−1.660	7.820	95	200410–201208
DJSC Hedge Fund Index	0.500	1.856	−6.550	−1.480	−0.220	0.740	1.730	2.340	4.060	−1.260	5.692	95	200410–201208

As explained earlier, arithmetic averages are sensitive toward outliers, and, in the presence of extreme returns, medians may provide a more accurate picture of the central tendency of a return distribution. The first observation that jumps out of Table 3.1 is that, with the exception of dedicated short bias and managed futures, all strategy indices have median returns that are greater than or equal to the mean returns. This observation implies that most hedge fund indices expose investors to extreme losses and the left tails of the hedge fund return distributions tend to be longer than the right tails. This is also evidenced by the prominence of negative skewness statistics that the indices exhibit. Skewness statistics vary between −2.677 and 0.025 for 11 out of 13 noninvestable strategy indices indicating that the asymmetries inherent in most hedge fund return distributions are relatively mild. The exceptions are equity market neutral and fixed income arbitrage indices that have skewness statistics of −11.820 and −4.439, respectively. These highly negative values are driven by the drastic losses that these two strategy indices experienced during the fall of 2008.

The composite DJCS Hedge Fund Index has a median return of 0.77%. Merger/risk arbitrage, equity market neutral, dedicated short bias, fixed income arbitrage, and managed futures indices that underperform the composite index in terms of their mean returns continue to underperform based on their median returns. However, some underperformers based on their mean returns such as convertible arbitrage, emerging markets, and multistrategy indices have higher median returns compared to that of the composite DJCS Index.

For all strategy indices, we observe that the standard deviation of returns is greater than the mean returns. The composite DJCS Hedge Fund Index has a standard deviation of 2.172%. Setting this figure as a yardstick, two groups of hedge fund indices stick out as being more volatile than the composite index. First, the equity hedge indices have standard deviations that vary between 2.862% and 4.901%. In other words, whether a hedge fund has a net long/short exposure or the fund claims to be equity market neutral is not enough to push its volatility below that of the composite index. Second, the standard deviations of the global macro, emerging markets, and managed futures indices are between 2.788% and 4.273% which is consistent with the idea these strategies are known to take directional bets. The event-driven and relative value-based indices have lower volatilities compared to that of the composite index.

The magnitudes of the extreme returns support our previous point that most hedge fund index return distributions have long tails on the left-hand side. With the exception of the long/short equity hedge, dedicated short bias and managed futures indices, the absolute values of the minimum returns are greater than the maximum returns for all strategy indices. We can emphasize this point by further adding that 10 out 13 strategy indices experience at least one monthly return worse than −10%, whereas only 4 out of 13 strategy indices experience at least one monthly return better than 10%. The best single monthly performance was 22.71% and exhibited by the dedicated short bias index during the LTCM bankruptcy in 1998. The worst single monthly performance was −40.45% and exhibited by the equity market neutral index during the credit crunch in 2008. As can be seen, these extreme returns are several standard deviations away from the mean returns. Thus, it is no surprise to find that most hedge fund indices have highly leptokurtic distributions. The three most leptokurtic indices are equity market neutral, fixed income arbitrage, and convertible arbitrage. The kurtosis statistics for these three indices are between 18.935 and 163.196.

Comparing the mean returns for noninvestable DJCS indices during the full sample period in Table 3.1 and the recent sample period in Table 3.2 makes it clear that the hedge fund industry had difficulties in generating returns as high as it used to generate earlier. For all strategy indices, the recent sample period exhibits lower mean and median returns compared to those in the full sample. The only exception to this pattern is the managed futures index which has a greater median return during the recent sample period. For the composite DJCS Hedge Fund Index, the mean monthly return drops to 0.50% from 0.72% and the median monthly return drops to 0.74% from 0.77%. The finding that the central tendency statistics for hedge fund indices were pulled downward may be due to both the adverse impact of the global financial crisis in 2008 and the increased difficulty in identifying and exploiting profitable arbitrage opportunities as the hedge fund industry accumulated more assets under management over time. In terms of the mean returns, the global macro and emerging market indices are the best performers during the recent sample period with average returns of 0.749% and 0.652%, respectively. The event-driven strategies also continue to be among the better performing strategies during the recent sample period with the exception of merger/risk arbitrage. The worst average performers are the dedicated short bias and long/short equity hedge indices with average returns of −0.441% and −0.061%, respectively.

The median returns tend to be higher than the mean returns and the skewness statistics tend to be negative during the recent sample period indicating the continued presence of long left tails and negative skewness in hedge fund return distributions. Twelve out of thirteen strategy indices exhibit negative skewness and the most negatively skewed strategy index is equity market neutral with a skewness statistic of −8.280. In contrast to all other indices, the dedicated short bias strategy index has positive skewness in the recent sample period. Emerging markets, global macro, and distressed restructuring indices are still the top three performers in terms of median returns, whereas dedicated short bias, merger/risk arbitrage, and managed futures strategies still have the lowest median returns. When we look at the extreme returns, we see that strategies under the equity hedge and relative value categories generated their lowest monthly returns in the recent sample period. Also, this period has witnessed the highest monthly performances of the strategies under the event driven and relative value categories. Kurtosis statistics encountered during the recent sample period are all lower than those for the full sample; however, hedge fund indices are still highly leptokurtic. The three most leptokurtic indices are still equity market neutral, fixed-income arbitrage, and convertible arbitrage. The final comparison between the full and the recent sample periods for the noninvestable DJCS indices can be made for the standard deviations. Although the average and median performances of these indices fell during the recent period, there is no corresponding uniform drop in the volatilities. Six out of thirteen strategy indices exhibit higher standard deviations in the latter sample period.

Figures 3.1−3.5 show how the monthly returns of the noninvestable DJCS indices evolved over time. One thing that is common to all figures is the lack of smoothness. The performance graphs cross over the horizontal axis repeatedly indicating that positive returns are commonly followed by negative returns and vice versa. Second, we observe that there are two major time periods where most hedge fund indices were badly hit. The first one corresponds to the

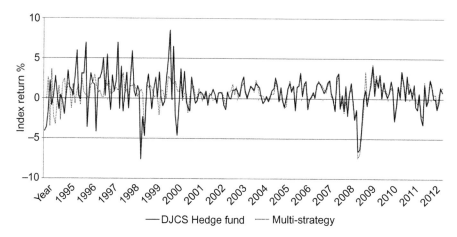

Figure 3.1 Historical performance of noninvestable DJCS hedge fund and multistrategy indices

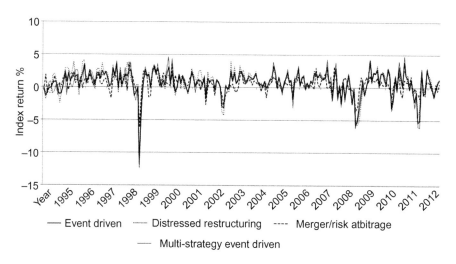

Figure 3.2 Historical performance of noninvestable DJCS event-driven, distressed restructuring, multistrategy event–driven, and merger/risk arbitrage indices

demise of, the Russian debt crisis in 1998, and the second one corresponds to the global financial crisis in 2008, triggered by problems in the subprime loan markets. The composite DJCS Hedge Fund Index experienced monthly returns lower than -5% during these two crisis periods. The event-driven indices in Figure 3.2 reacted more adversely to the LTCM meltdown, whereas the equity hedge indices in Figure 3.3 reacted more adversely to the recent credit crunch. In fact, the dedicated short bias strategy was able to produce positive returns

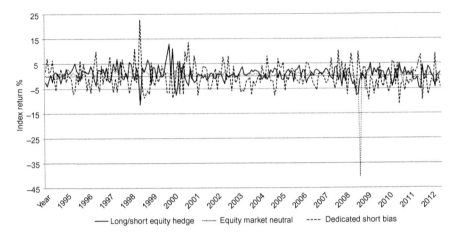

Figure 3.3 Historical performance of noninvestable DJCS long/short equity hedge, equity market neutral, and dedicated short bias indices

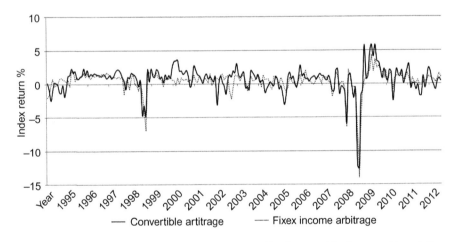

Figure 3.4 Historical performance of noninvestable DJCS convertible arbitrage and fixed-income arbitrage indices

in both periods of market turmoil due to the nature of its trading strategy. Relative value strategies in Figure 3.4 were more sensitive toward the 2008 crisis and experienced returns lower than −10%. The opposite was true for the global macro, managed futures, and emerging markets indices in Figure 3.5. Due to the Russian debt crisis in 1998, the emerging markets index experienced a monthly loss of about −23%. Figure 3.5 also shows that the upward and downward swings of the

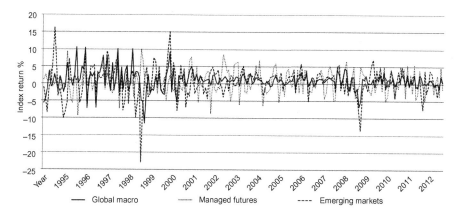

Figure 3.5 Historical performance of noninvestable DJCS global macro, managed futures, and emerging markets indices

emerging markets index was more pronounced compared to the global macro and managed futures indices.

The fact that the hedge fund indices generated highly negative returns during the two major market crashes is troublesome in terms of portfolio diversification. It may be the case that hedge funds are focused on absolute returns and their performances are, on average, weakly correlated with those of traditional asset classes. However, Figures 3.1–3.5 show that almost all hedge fund indices become strongly correlated with each other and traditional market indices during market downturns. These are exactly the instances during which investing in hedge funds should payoff in terms of diversification; however, the figures suggest that hedge fund indices do not fulfill their insurance roles when they are most needed.

One final comment to be made about the figures is related to the correlations between the returns of strategies that can be grouped under the same category based on the classification system in Chapter 2. First, the correlation between the composite DJCS Hedge Fund Index and the multistrategy index is equal to 0.51. Second, the event-driven strategies in Figure 3.2 tend to move in tandem, and we calculate the correlations between monthly returns between these four strategy indices to be between 0.59 and 0.96. Third, the equity hedge indices in Figure 3.3 do not seem to be strongly correlated. This is to be expected since the average long/short equity hedge fund has a long exposure, dedicated short bias funds have short exposures, and equity market neutral funds try to maintain zero exposure toward the equity markets. Unreported correlation statistics show that the dedicated short bias index is negatively correlated with the two other indices under the equity hedge category. The long/short equity hedge and equity market neutral indices have a correlation of 0.23, which is also low in comparison to the within-group correlations exhibited by other strategy categories. Fourth, the convertible arbitrage and fixed income arbitrage strategies in Figure 3.4 also seem to be reaching their peaks and troughs roughly around the same times. The correlation between these two relative value-based indices is 0.88. Finally, the global macro, managed futures, and emerging markets strategies in Figure 3.5 are all directional strategies by nature; however, their correlations are not substantial.

Table 3.3 presents descriptive statistics for 10 investable strategy indices and the investable DJCS AllHedge Composite Index. The database does not calculate investable indices for distressed restructuring, merger/risk arbitrage, and multistrategy event-driven strategies. Since investable indices only consider those hedge funds that investors are free to invest capital to and redeem capital from, they are more likely to represent the actual returns that a new investor can realize by investing in hedge funds.

The most important observation from Table 3.3 is that the mean returns for investable indices are lower than those for the noninvestable indices in Table 3.2. For example, the noninvestable DJCS Hedge Fund Index has an average return of 0.50% in the recent sample period, whereas the investable DJCS AllHedge Index has an average return of only 0.23%. The only exception to this pattern is the dedicated short bias strategy. This finding is not unexpected because we noted earlier that many well-performing hedge funds are closed to new capital contributions so that their returns are not diluted and funds that have lock-up and redemption restrictions may have performance advantages in terms of being able to include more illiquid assets in their portfolios.

There are no drastic differences between the rankings among noninvestable indices and investable indices. The only major change that sticks out is that the global macro and managed futures strategies trade places. The managed futures index which has the seventh highest mean return among the noninvestable indices is the top performer among the investable indices with an average monthly return of

Table 3.3 Descriptive Statistics for DJCS Investable Indices (Recent Sample)

	Mean	SD	Min	10%	25%	Median	75%	90%	Max	Skew	Kurt	#Obs	Data Interval
Event driven	0.349	2.342	−8.210	−2.230	−1.100	0.640	1.850	2.880	5.590	−0.788	4.555	95	200410–201208
Long/short equity hedge	0.252	2.661	−10.470	−3.260	−1.240	1.010	2.020	2.820	4.440	−1.447	6.102	95	200410–201208
Equity market neutral	−0.142	2.939	−17.890	−1.900	−0.800	0.210	0.720	1.610	9.240	−2.788	19.276	95	200410–201208
Dedicated short bias	−0.391	4.715	−15.940	−5.210	−3.360	−0.750	2.950	5.610	12.100	0.003	3.706	95	200410–201208
Convertible arbitrage	0.197	3.510	−20.180	−1.900	−0.480	0.640	1.420	2.490	6.460	−3.544	21.025	95	200410–201208
Fixed-income arbitrage	−0.197	2.969	−20.420	−1.220	−0.350	0.290	0.860	1.230	10.050	−3.825	27.745	95	200410–201208
Global macro	0.177	2.639	−13.780	−2.570	−0.530	0.330	1.650	2.380	7.790	−1.766	11.805	95	200410–201208
Emerging markets	0.420	4.187	−20.650	−5.060	−1.270	1.190	2.710	5.070	7.790	−1.631	8.744	95	200410–201208
Managed futures	0.497	2.929	−5.970	−3.350	−1.980	0.570	2.830	4.480	7.190	−0.076	2.173	95	200410–201208
Multistrategy	0.234	2.300	−13.430	−1.560	−0.290	0.560	1.340	1.900	7.350	−2.688	17.410	95	200410–201208
DJCS AllHedge Index	0.230	2.119	−10.450	−1.810	−0.630	0.750	1.600	2.170	3.390	−2.172	10.842	95	200410–201208

0.497%. The global macro index which is the top performer among the noninvestable indices has only the seventh highest mean return among the investable indices with an average monthly return of 0.177%. After the managed futures strategy, the emerging markets and event-driven strategies have the highest mean returns which is similar to the results from Table 3.2. The worst performers also stay the same. The dedicated short bias, fixed income arbitrage, and equity market neutral strategies produce the worst results, with average returns that are between −0.391% and −0.142%.

The median returns of all investable indices are greater than the mean returns with the exception of the dedicated short bias index. This finding highlights the fact that investable hedge fund indices also have long left tails. Consequently, all strategy indices except the dedicated short bias index have negative skewness statistics that range from −3.825 to −0.076. The DJCS AllHedge Index is also negatively skewed with a skewness statistic of −2.172. One final note to be made about the median rankings is that, although the worst three performers are the same as those for the mean rankings, the long/short equity index replaces the managed futures index in the top three.

The standard deviations of all investable indices are several times higher than their means. Moreover, the volatility of the investable indices for 8 out 10 strategies is higher than the volatility of the corresponding noninvestable indices, with the exception of the equity market neutral and managed futures strategies. Consistent with the prominence of long left tails in the return distributions, the absolute value of the minimum index return is greater than the maximum return for all investable indices except managed futures. The minimum monthly returns are quite substantial and convertible arbitrage, fixed arbitrage, and emerging markets are three strategy indices that experienced a monthly return lower than −20%. In contrast, there are only two strategy indices that experienced a monthly return greater than 10%. We also see that the minimum returns of investable indices are even lower than those of the noninvestable indices, with the exception of the equity market neutral strategy. This finding indicates that the investable hedge funds were even more harshly beaten by the 2008 crisis compared to their noninvestable counterparts. The extreme returns of all investable hedge fund indices lie far away from their means indicating the presence of fat tails. The large kurtosis statistics confirm this conjecture. The fixed income arbitrage and convertible arbitrage strategies lead the bunch with kurtosis statistics of 27.745 and 21.025, respectively. The composite investable hedge fund index is also highly leptokurtic with a kurtosis statistic of 10.842.

Figures 3.6–3.9 show how the monthly returns of the investable DJCS indices evolved over time. There are two general conclusions we can draw from these figures. First, all the investable hedge fund indices reacted negatively in the face of the 2008 financial crisis. The minimum monthly returns of all investable hedge fund indices belong to this period, and these minimum returns vary

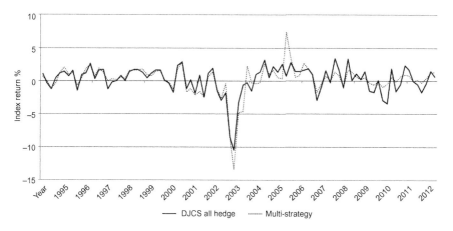

Figure 3.6 Historical performance of investable DJCS all hedge and multistrategy indices

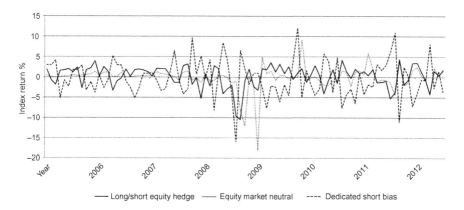

Figure 3.7 Historical performance of investable DJCS long/short equity hedge, equity market neutral, and dedicated short bias indices

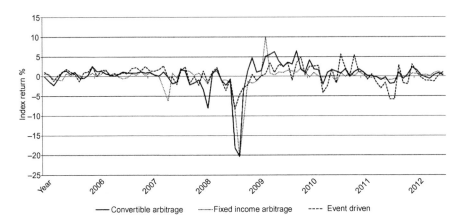

Figure 3.8 Historical performance of investable DJCS convertible arbitrage, fixed income arbitrage and event driven indices

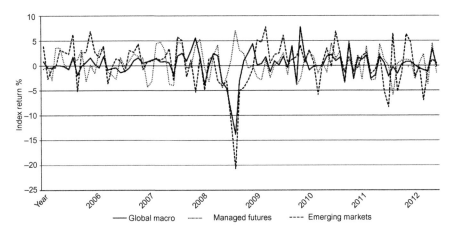

Figure 3.9 Historical performance of investable DJCS global macro, managed futures, and emerging markets indices

between −10% and −20%. As explained before, this observation has negative implications regarding the diversification benefits of investing in hedge funds. The only strategy that managed to escape the credit crunch was managed futures. In October 2010, a month which turned out to be exceptionally dismal for all investable indices, the managed futures index posted a monthly return of 7.19%. Second, for all investable indices, about one-third of the months during the recent sample exhibit negative returns. This proportion is even higher for the dedicated short bias strategy, which posted negative monthly returns during more than half of the sample period. The implication is that, although hedge funds are absolute return oriented by nature, they are not able to generate such absolute returns consistently.

In terms of within-group correlations, the findings are similar to those for the noninvestable indices. First, the correlation between the DJCS AllHedge Index and the multistrategy index is substantial and is equal to 0.84. Second, in Figure 3.7, the dedicated short bias strategy again has negative correlations with the two other equity hedge strategies. However, the correlation between the long/short equity hedge and equity market neutral indices increases to 0.50. Third, the two relative value strategies in Figure 3.8, namely convertible arbitrage and fixed income arbitrage, are again highly correlated with a correlation coefficient of 0.84. Finally, although the correlation between the managed futures index and the two other indices in Figure 3.9 is close to zero, emerging markets and global macro indices tend to move together and have a correlation coefficient of 0.62.

3.3.2 HFR Hedge Fund Indices

We present the descriptive statistics for noninvestable indices provided by HFR in Tables 3.4 and 3.5. Our aim is not to compare these statistics with those of the DJCS indices because we already know that the two databases differ from each other based on the hedge fund universe they focus on and their weighting scheme for individual hedge fund returns. Moreover, the sample period for HFR indices begins 4 years prior to that of DJCS indices. The primary goal of this section is exploring whether the general trends we have highlighted for DJCS indices also apply to HFR indices. Again, we provide two sets of summary statistics for the noninvestable indices, one for the full sample period in Table 3.4 and one for a more recent sample period in Table 3.5. The index data begins at January 1990 in Table 3.4 with the exception of a few strategy indices that start as late as January 1995. In Table 3.5, we initiate the recent sample period in January 2005 because the investable indices, whose descriptive statistics are reported in Table 3.6, begin at this date. Again, we follow this convention to be able to make meaningful comparisons between noninvestable and investable HFR indices.

In Table 3.4, the mean return of HFRI Fund Weighted Composite Index is equal to 0.898% per month. For DJCS indices, we have seen that the global macro strategy was among the top performers and this

Table 3.4 Descriptive Statistics for HFR Noninvestable Indices (Full Sample)

	Mean	SD	Min	10%	25%	Median	75%	90%	Max	Skew	Kurt	#Obs	Data Interval
Event driven	0.932	1.995	−8.900	−1.412	0.002	1.260	2.085	3.036	5.130	−1.275	6.773	272	199001–201208
Distressed restructuring	0.959	1.908	−8.500	−0.850	0.116	1.110	2.020	2.840	7.060	−1.003	7.606	272	199001–201208
Merger/risk arbitrage	0.699	1.178	−6.460	−0.452	0.219	0.860	1.423	1.894	3.116	−2.086	11.637	272	199001–201208
Long/short equity hedge	1.033	2.682	−9.458	−2.204	−0.576	1.191	2.595	4.090	10.880	−0.253	4.680	272	199001–201208
Equity market neutral	0.558	0.947	−2.872	−0.442	0.036	0.554	1.053	1.800	3.590	−0.272	4.467	272	199001–201208
Quantitative directional	1.022	3.777	−13.340	−3.725	−1.416	1.468	3.389	5.400	10.740	−0.439	3.699	272	199001–201208
Dedicated short bias	0.129	5.437	−21.210	−5.706	−2.945	−0.194	3.577	6.640	22.840	0.203	5.091	272	199001–201208
Energy/basic materials	1.366	5.335	−17.089	−4.050	−1.708	1.518	3.987	7.570	19.830	0.048	4.500	212	199501–201208
Technology/healthcare	1.238	4.757	−15.160	−4.270	−1.197	1.106	3.440	6.558	21.560	0.441	5.929	260	199101–201208
Relative value	0.823	1.277	−8.031	−0.450	0.330	0.903	1.494	2.040	5.720	−2.118	16.188	272	199001–201208
Convertible arbitrage	0.712	1.934	−16.010	−1.034	0.183	0.980	1.510	2.110	9.744	−3.007	30.447	272	199001–201208
Fixed-income corporate arbitrage	0.656	1.915	−10.646	−1.088	0.050	0.822	1.602	2.420	9.540	−1.323	10.656	272	199001–201208
Fixed-income asset-backed-arbitrage	0.776	1.184	−9.240	−0.320	0.534	0.884	1.355	1.749	3.424	−3.529	26.759	236	199301–201208
Yield alternatives	0.666	2.150	−8.787	−1.481	−0.612	0.745	1.966	3.189	6.690	−0.940	5.986	224	199401–201208
Multistrategy relative value	0.685	1.276	−8.397	−0.659	0.244	0.820	1.289	1.800	5.340	−2.060	15.921	272	199001–201208

Global macro	1.001	2.193	−6.400	−1.250	−0.478	0.746	2.155	3.710	7.880	0.511	3.893	272	199001–201208
Systematic diversified	0.915	2.156	−4.410	−1.810	−0.619	0.934	2.436	3.419	6.490	0.120	2.663	272	199001–201208
Emerging markets	1.056	4.142	−21.020	−3.961	−1.207	1.531	3.591	5.420	14.800	−0.832	6.461	272	199001–201208
Fund of funds composite	0.603	1.691	−7.470	−1.414	−0.215	0.754	1.566	2.300	6.850	−0.662	6.741	272	199001–201208
Fund of funds conservative	0.516	1.153	−5.910	−0.750	0.142	0.694	1.217	1.520	3.960	−1.675	10.230	272	199001–201208
Fund of funds diversified	0.569	1.738	−7.750	−1.447	−0.226	0.687	1.513	2.350	7.730	−0.444	6.844	272	199001–201208
Fund of funds market defensive	0.655	1.699	−5.420	−1.353	−0.509	0.625	1.564	2.875	7.380	0.188	3.862	272	199001–201208
Fund of funds strategic	0.792	2.515	−12.110	−2.191	−0.620	1.053	2.099	3.617	9.475	−0.459	6.244	272	199001–201208
HFRI Fund Weighted Composite Index	0.898	2.034	−8.700	−1.560	−0.190	1.176	2.100	3.170	7.650	−0.689	5.319	272	199001–201208

Table 3.5 Descriptive Statistics for HFR Noninvestable Indices (Recent Sample)

	Mean	SD	Min	10%	25%	Median	75%	90%	Max	Skew	Kurt	#Obs	Data Interval
Event driven	0.427	2.066	−8.191	−1.798	−0.485	0.926	1.710	2.519	4.743	−1.236	5.826	92	200501−201208
Distressed restructuring	0.430	2.058	−7.934	−1.865	−0.253	0.815	1.625	2.441	5.550	−1.325	6.286	92	200501−201208
Merger/risk arbitrage	0.430	1.011	−2.896	−0.858	−0.055	0.627	1.130	1.467	3.116	−0.692	4.119	92	200501−201208
Long/short equity hedge	0.329	2.756	−9.458	−2.845	−1.266	0.815	2.186	3.176	6.374	−0.870	4.459	92	200501−01208
Equity market neutral	0.180	0.889	−2.872	−0.766	−0.232	0.347	0.747	1.122	1.845	−1.358	5.550	92	200501−201208
Quantitative directional	0.363	2.883	−9.145	−3.681	−1.438	0.783	2.612	3.577	5.813	−0.741	3.414	92	200501−201208
Dedicated short bias	−0.198	3.466	−10.086	−4.758	−2.336	−0.299	2.468	4.333	9.577	0.007	3.031	92	200501−201208
Energy/basic materials	0.436	4.618	−17.089	−4.101	−2.308	0.970	3.649	5.257	10.078	−1.131	5.425	92	200501−201208
Technology/healthcare	0.591	2.523	−6.082	−3.160	−1.095	0.905	2.427	3.379	6.002	−0.498	2.945	92	200501−201208
Relative value	0.520	1.603	−8.031	−0.844	−0.048	0.770	1.379	1.752	3.933	−2.388	12.835	92	200501−201208
Convertible arbitrage	0.417	3.020	−16.010	−1.960	−0.701	0.761	1.454	2.762	9.744	−2.020	14.405	92	200501−201208
Fixed-income corporate arbitrage	0.372	2.034	−10.646	−1.808	−0.145	0.729	1.287	2.219	4.470	−2.065	11.642	92	200501−201208
Fixed-income asset-backed arbitrage	0.693	0.966	−3.073	−0.480	0.430	0.718	1.147	1.749	3.424	−0.639	5.669	92	200501−201208
Yield alternatives	0.402	2.327	−8.787	−1.902	−0.777	0.801	1.754	2.745	5.373	−1.336	6.218	92	200501−201208
Multistrategy relative value	0.338	1.645	−8.397	−1.199	−0.159	0.583	0.990	2.065	3.886	−2.321	12.994	92	200501−201208
Global macro	0.428	1.460	−2.624	−1.302	−0.643	0.358	1.484	2.357	4.219	0.266	2.504	92	200501−201208
Systematic diversified	0.690	2.502	−4.410	−2.548	−1.112	0.443	2.539	3.419	6.490	0.238	2.580	92	200501−201208

Emerging markets	0.598	3.771	−14.446	−4.138	−1.280	1.393	3.023	4.664	9.618	−0.997	5.226	92	200501–201208
Fund of funds composite	0.187	1.749	−6.536	−2.177	−0.577	0.564	1.494	1.787	3.324	−1.281	5.614	92	200501–201208
Fund of funds conservative	0.136	1.413	−5.910	−1.795	−0.291	0.474	1.062	1.347	2.420	−1.969	8.546	92	200501–201208
Fund of funds diversifed	0.194	1.678	−6.530	−2.183	−0.571	0.493	1.403	1.803	3.066	−1.315	5.734	92	200501–201208
Fund of funds market defensive	0.361	1.613	−3.218	−1.629	−0.668	0.343	1.494	2.193	4.926	0.163	2.853	92	200501–201208
Fund of funds strategic	0.215	2.188	−7.660	−2.717	−0.890	0.602	1.873	2.372	4.247	−1.130	4.889	92	200501–201208
HFRI Fund Weighted Composite Index	0.4064	2.020	−6.842	−2.237	−0.813	0.706	1.799	2.686	5.147	−0.893	4.581	92	200501–201208

Table 3.6 Descriptive Statistics for HFR Investable Indices

Panel A: Recent Sample

	Mean	SD	Min	10%	25%	Median	75%	90%	Max	Skew	Kurt	#Obs	Data Interval
Event driven	0.114	1.931	−7.526	−2.050	−0.735	0.611	1.471	2.110	3.153	−1.473	6.414	92	200501−201208
Distressed restructuring	−0.249	2.291	−11.688	−2.369	−0.894	−0.029	1.086	1.866	3.494	−2.145	10.675	92	200501−201208
Merger/risk arbitrage	0.380	1.009	−2.850	−0.852	−0.124	0.579	0.972	1.411	2.322	−0.929	4.099	92	200501−201208
Credit arbitrage	0.624	1.243	−2.786	−0.947	0.025	0.668	1.330	1.997	4.361	0.026	4.086	92	200501−201208
Activist	0.611	4.532	−16.302	−4.937	−1.898	1.078	3.613	5.959	9.682	−0.795	4.425	92	200501−201208
Special situations	0.127	2.278	−10.987	−2.399	−0.783	0.599	1.711	2.346	3.488	−2.122	10.424	92	200501−201208
Multistrategy event driven	0.550	3.014	−14.873	−1.527	−0.448	0.835	1.867	3.369	8.992	−1.987	12.794	92	200501−201208
Long/short equity hedge	−0.088	2.492	−9.987	−3.069	−1.360	0.194	1.534	2.699	5.187	−1.109	5.642	92	200501−201208
Equity market neutral	−0.043	1.184	−3.782	−1.523	−0.573	0.029	0.825	1.317	2.455	−0.514	3.633	92	200501−201208
Quantitative directional	0.375	2.032	−4.718	−2.064	−0.578	0.345	1.317	3.102	6.462	0.074	3.717	92	200501−201208
Dedicated short bias	−0.343	3.718	−11.801	−5.027	−2.955	−0.254	2.457	4.479	8.462	−0.103	2.967	92	200501−201208
Fundamental growth	0.456	3.230	−8.374	−3.800	−1.650	0.549	2.676	4.636	6.970	−0.228	2.639	92	200501−201208
Fundamental value	−0.016	2.525	−8.893	−2.815	−0.958	0.456	1.534	2.415	4.927	−1.318	5.555	92	200501−201208
Energy/basic materials	0.439	4.020	−16.253	−3.735	−1.894	0.827	2.564	4.945	10.293	−0.708	5.760	92	200501−201208
Technology/healthcare	0.527	2.099	−6.268	−1.822	−0.703	0.501	1.761	2.929	6.545	−0.294	4.133	92	200501−201208
Multistrategy equity hedge	0.546	3.800	−10.506	−5.297	−1.607	1.095	3.041	4.263	8.721	−0.532	3.235	92	200501−201208
Relative value	0.099	2.633	−14.111	−2.257	−0.510	0.380	1.222	2.334	6.814	−2.298	13.173	92	200501−201208
Convertible arbitrage	−0.296	4.578	−34.683	−1.900	−0.789	0.314	1.342	2.342	6.735	−5.212	37.592	92	200501−201208
Fixed-income corporate arbitrage	0.372	2.065	−12.736	−1.497	−0.030	0.784	1.448	1.925	3.772	−3.355	20.325	92	200501−201208
Fixed-income sovereign arbitrage	0.296	2.547	−15.938	−1.261	−0.243	0.584	1.337	2.096	5.152	−3.557	22.003	92	200501−201208

Fixed-income asset-backed arbitrage	0.922	1.099	−3.338	−0.322	0.485	0.798	1.612	2.261	3.262	−0.688	4.815	92	200501−201208
Yield alternatives	0.641	3.113	−13.246	−4.122	−0.593	1.228	2.621	3.905	6.810	−1.293	6.225	92	200501−201208
Energy infrastructure	0.885	3.340	−12.927	−3.781	−0.770	1.454	3.125	4.554	7.748	−0.970	5.059	92	200501−201208
Real estate	0.171	2.416	−8.247	−3.515	−0.918	0.607	1.584	2.966	4.688	−0.820	3.797	92	200501−201208
Volatility	0.267	1.639	−7.678	−1.497	−0.511	0.740	1.208	1.751	2.758	−1.949	8.598	92	200501−201208
Multistrategy relative value	0.657	1.912	−9.247	−0.879	−0.118	0.652	1.348	2.169	7.100	−0.989	11.092	92	200501−201208
Global macro	0.074	2.380	−7.379	−2.520	−1.380	0.069	1.446	3.132	8.536	0.257	4.542	92	200501−201208
Discretionary thematic	0.621	2.729	−9.102	−2.043	−0.703	0.388	2.323	4.486	6.306	−0.409	4.271	92	200501−201208
Systematic diversified	0.554	3.119	−5.125	−3.403	−1.974	0.611	2.770	4.431	11.556	0.494	3.352	92	200501−201208
Active trading	0.511	1.401	−5.140	−1.052	−0.221	−0.029	1.309	2.218	3.783	−0.606	5.052	92	200501−201208
Currency	0.015	1.494	−4.656	−1.840	−0.800	0.579	0.836	1.837	4.146	−0.157	3.674	92	200501−201208
Commodity	0.555	2.259	−4.359	−1.806	−0.867	0.668	1.664	3.358	9.108	0.668	4.232	92	200501−201208
Agriculture	0.357	2.469	−4.158	−2.782	−1.083	1.078	1.478	3.021	8.395	0.895	4.599	92	200501−201208
Energy	0.245	3.626	−15.033	−2.912	−1.703	0.599	2.245	4.587	10.072	−0.832	7.019	68	200701−201208
Metals	1.361	6.862	−17.245	−6.987	−3.495	0.835	6.166	9.375	18.555	−0.043	3.160	92	200501−201208
Multistrategy global macro	0.543	1.835	−4.310	−1.701	−0.658	0.194	1.769	2.562	6.229	0.176	3.702	92	200501−201208
Emerging markets	0.911	3.071	−12.901	−2.042	−0.590	0.029	2.877	4.030	8.202	−1.099	7.289	80	200601−201208
HFRX Global Hedge Fund Index	0.017	1.917	−9.347	−2.413	−0.903	0.345	1.330	1.722	3.150	−1.852	9.073	92	200501−201208
HFRX equal weighted strategies	0.018	1.700	−9.930	−1.686	−0.500	−0.254	1.132	1.552	2.277	−2.767	15.398	92	200501−201208
HFRX absolute return	−0.079	1.050	−4.393	−1.214	−0.580	0.549	0.545	1.216	1.814	−1.301	6.175	92	200501−201208
HFRX market directional	0.035	2.957	−13.944	−3.035	−1.322	0.456	1.869	3.101	5.198	−1.612	7.855	92	200501−201208

Panel B: Full Sample

	Mean	SD	Min	10%	25%	Median	75%	90%	Max	Skew	Kurt	#Obs	Data Interval
Event driven	0.423	1.970	−9.020	−1.982	−0.558	0.780	1.574	2.440	4.790	−1.452	7.479	176	199801–201208
Distressed restructuring	0.303	2.141	−11.688	−1.640	−0.483	0.410	1.488	2.580	6.110	−1.645	10.141	176	199801–201208
Merger/risk arbitrage	0.469	1.064	−4.560	−0.779	0.007	0.611	1.155	1.530	3.290	−1.114	6.113	176	199801–201208
Long/short equity hedge	0.494	2.501	−9.987	−2.488	−0.840	0.575	1.763	3.290	9.780	−0.341	6.017	176	199801–201208
Equity market neutral	0.080	1.168	−3.782	−1.473	−0.569	0.150	0.857	1.550	2.920	−0.335	3.429	176	199801–201208
Relative value	0.369	2.102	−14.111	−1.400	−0.055	0.593	1.205	1.860	6.814	−2.740	18.528	176	199801–201208
Convertible arbitrage	0.168	3.424	−34.683	−1.592	−0.343	0.628	1.349	2.120	6.735	−6.828	65.763	176	199801–201208
Volatility	0.327	1.563	−7.678	−1.428	−0.245	0.755	1.208	1.751	2.758	−2.083	9.515	104	200401–201208
Global macro	0.528	2.546	−7.379	−2.240	−0.996	0.335	1.781	3.777	8.536	0.314	4.078	176	199801–201208
HFRX global hedge fund	0.458	1.928	−9.347	−1.687	−0.431	0.470	1.484	2.361	5.950	−0.664	7.682	176	199801–201208
HFRX equal weighted strategies	0.366	1.488	−9.930	−1.110	−0.180	0.539	1.172	1.755	3.278	−2.606	16.853	176	199801–201208
HFRX absolute return	0.252	1.062	−4.393	−0.899	−0.237	0.349	1.035	1.413	2.308	−1.193	6.115	176	199801–201208
HFRX market directional	0.499	2.711	−13.944	−2.577	−0.871	0.794	2.050	3.261	6.273	−1.346	7.803	176	199801–201208

is also true for HFRI indices. The global macro and systematic diversified indices have an average monthly return of 1.001% and 0.915%, respectively. The indices under the event-driven category also have favorable average performances as event-driven and distressed restructuring indices generated mean returns of 0.932% and 0.959%, respectively. The merger/arbitrage index again constitutes an exception and underperforms the noninvestable composite index with a mean return of 0.699%. The performances of the indices under the equity hedge category were heterogeneous for DJCS indices and this continues to be the case. On the one hand, the long/short equity hedge index has a mean return of 1.033% and the quantitative directional index, which is based on maintaining varying exposures to the market based on the economic outlook, has a mean return of 1.022%. Moreover, the equity hedge indices that are oriented toward specific sectors are the top average performers among all strategy indices. The energy/basic materials and the technology/healthcare indices have average returns of 1.366% and 1.238%, respectively. On the other hand, the dedicated short bias and equity market neutral indices underperform the HFRI Fund Weighted Composite Index with average returns of 0.129 and 0.558, respectively. The indices under the relative value category have average performances that are below the composite index. The six indices in this group differentiate among each other based on the particular financial instruments they focus on and their average performances are in a narrow band between 0.656% and 0.823%. The emerging markets index is again a decent performer with a mean return of 1.056%. Table 3.4 also presents descriptive statistics for five distinct noninvestable fund of hedge fund indices. The constituent funds for these five indices differ from each other based on their market exposures and risk-taking behaviors as explained in Chapter 2. All the fund of fund indices underperform HFRI Fund Weighted Composite Index with the conservative funds of funds index being the worst performer with a mean return of 0.516% and the strategic funds of funds index being the best performer with a mean return of 0.792%.

The median returns are greater than the mean returns for most of the HFRI indices with notable exceptions being the dedicated short bias and global macro indices. The return distribution for the market defensive funds of funds index also has a higher median than its mean consistent with the fact that market defensive funds of funds generally invest in hedge funds that follow short-biased strategies. In line with the finding that most indices have median returns that exceed the means, 18 out of 24 noninvestable indices exhibit negative skewness. The most negative skewness is displayed by the indices under the relative value category, especially the fixed-income asset backed and convertible arbitrage indices that have skewness statistics of −3.520 and −3.007, respectively. The most positive skewness belongs to the global macro index with a statistic of 0.511 which is relatively mild. HFRI Fund Weighted Composite Index is also negatively skewed with a statistic of −0.689.

We had pointed out that, for the DJCS indices, the most volatile strategies are the ones under the equity hedge category and some directional strategies such as global macro and emerging markets. These results are generally intact for HFRI indices. The composite noninvestable HFRI Index has a standard deviation of 2.034%. The global macro and emerging markets indices are more volatile than the composite index with standard deviations of 2.193% and 4.142%, respectively. However, the most volatile indices are encountered under the equity hedge category with dedicated short bias and quantitative directional strategies having standard deviations of 5.437% and 3.777%, respectively. Moreover, the sector-oriented equity hedge indices are very volatile with standard deviations of 5.335% and 4.757% for the energy/basic materials and technology/healthcare indices, respectively. The only exception is the equity market neutral index which has a volatility of only 0.947% which is in line with the idea that this strategy aims to maintain a low exposure toward market movements. The indices under the event-driven and the relative value categories are generally less volatile than the composite index. The merger/risk arbitrage and the fixed-income asset-backed arbitrage indices stick out as the least volatile indices among these two categories with standard deviations of 1.178% and 1.184%, respectively. The fund of funds indices are also less volatile than the HFRI Fund Weighted Composite Index with the only exception of the strategic funds of funds index.

In contrast to the DJCS indices, the absolute values of the minimum returns are not uniformly greater than the maximum returns for HFRI indices. For example, all indices grouped under equity hedge except the quantitative directional index have higher peaks compared to their troughs. The same pattern holds for the global and systematic diversified indices as well as the market defensive funds of funds index. As mentioned earlier, these indices are also the ones with positive skewness. The most severe negative returns are experienced by the dedicated short bias and emerging markets indices with minimum monthly returns of -21.210% and -21.020%, respectively. The highest maximum monthly returns also belong to these two indices along with the two sector-oriented equity hedge indices. Such extreme returns drive the distributions of all HFRI indices to be leptokurtic. Two indices grouped under relative value, the convertible arbitrage and fixed-income asset backed indices, deserve special attention with their kurtosis statistics of 30.447 and 26.759. HFRI Fund Weighted Composite Index is also leptokurtic with a kurtosis statistic of 5.319.

Table 3.5 presents descriptive statistics for HFRI indices for the recent sample period that begins from January 2005. The first observation is that the mean returns are lower than those for the full sample period, indicating that the profitability of the hedge fund industry dropped over time. For example, the mean return of the HFRI Fund Weighted Composite Index more than halved from 0.898 to 0.406. The systematic diversified index is still one of the top performing indices with a mean return of 0.690. The event-driven and the distressed restructuring indices still perform a little better than the composite index; however, the most notable observation here is that the performance gap between the merger/risk arbitrage strategy and the other event-driven strategies has closed. There is a drop in the performances of most of the indices grouped under the equity hedge category. The dedicated short bias and the equity market neutral strategies continue to be the worst performers with average returns of -0.198% and 0.180%. On top of this, the long/short equity hedge and the quantitative directional strategies now lag behind the composite HFRI Index. It is only the sector-oriented equity hedge funds that have a superior average performance compared to the composite HFRI Index. In contrast to the equity hedge category, the relative value category improves its performance. All of the indices under this category had lower mean returns compared to the HFRI Index in the full sample; however, the relative value index has a mean return of 0.520% in the recent sample and the fixed income asset-backed arbitrage strategy has the highest mean return among all indices reported in Table 3.5, with an average return of 0.693%. The emerging markets index is still a top contender with an average return of 0.598% and the fund of funds indices continue to underperform the HFRI Fund Weighted Composite Index. The highest mean return among the fund of fund indices belongs to the market defensive strategy and even this index has a lower average return than 18 strategy-specific indices. This last finding may be driven by the aforementioned double-fee structure imposed by funds of hedge funds.

The median returns are still generally greater than the mean returns with the same exceptions of dedicated short bias and market defensive funds of funds indices as well as the global macro and systematic diversified indices. All other HFRI indices have negatively skewed return distributions. The most positive skewness statistic is only 0.266 and it belongs to the global macro index. The most negatively skewed indices are again in the relative value category and 4 out of 6 indices grouped here have skewness statistics below -2. HFRI Fund Weighted Composite Index is also negatively skewed with a statistic of -0.893.

The standard deviation of the noninvestable composite index is equal to 2.02% which is very close to its value in the full sample period. There are two categories that exhibit significant changes in the recent sample period. The indices under the relative value category display increases in their standard deviations except the fixed income asset-backed arbitrage index and the indices under the equity hedge category display decreases in their standard deviations except the long/short equity hedge index. Despite such volatility decreases in the equity hedge category, the dedicated short bias and quantitative directional indices continue to be among the most volatile indices with standard deviations of 3.466% and 2.883%, respectively. A similar situation exists for the sector-oriented equity hedge and emerging markets indices whose volatilities are smaller in the recent sample period but still higher than most other indices. The fund of funds indices are still less volatile than the noninvestable composite index with the only exception being the strategic fund of funds index.

In the recent sample period, the tendency of the absolute value of the minimum index returns to be higher than the maximum returns is stronger compared to the full sample period. For example, in contrast to Table 3.4, all indices under the equity hedge category have deeper troughs compared to their peaks in Table 3.5. The exceptions to this pattern are the global macro, systematic diversified, and market directional funds of funds indices. The most negative monthly returns belong to the energy/basic materials, convertible arbitrage, and emerging markets indices with minimum between −17.089% and −14.446%. The highest monthly returns also belong to these three indices with maximum between 9.618% and 10.078%. Although the kurtosis statistics decrease for 20 out of 24 indices reported in Tables 3.4 and 3.5, most of the hedge fund indices continue to be leptokurtic in the recent sample period. The least leptokurtic indices belong to the global macro and systematic diversified strategies with kurtosis values equal to 2.504 and 2.580, respectively. The highest kurtosis statistics are encountered in the relative value category and four indices in this group have kurtosis statistics exceeding 10 with the most leptokurtic distribution being that of the convertible arbitrage index. The HFRI Fund Weighted Composite Index is also leptokurtic with a kurtosis value of 4.581.

Figures 3.10−3.16 show how the monthly returns of the noninvestable composite HFRI indices evolved over time. The first observation is that almost all hedge fund indices were adversely affected by the Russian debt crisis in 1998 and the global financial crisis in 2008. Figure 3.10 shows that the HFRI Fund Weighted Composite Index experienced monthly value losses well above 5% during these two crisis periods. Another observation is that the performance graph of the composite index has frequent upward and downward swings. We find that the composite index experienced negative returns in about 30% of the months during the full sample period, indicating the difficulty of maintaining an absolute return focus. HFRI

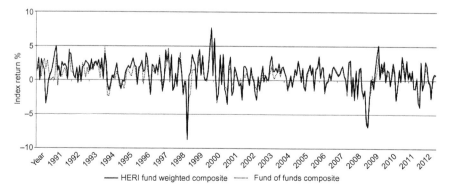

Figure 3.10 Historical performance of noninvestable HFRI fund weighted composite and fund of funds composite indices

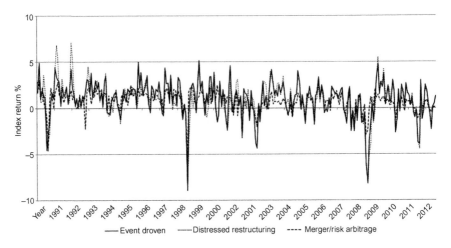

Figure 3.11 Historical performance of noninvestable HFRI event-driven, distressed restructuring, and merger/risk arbitrage indices

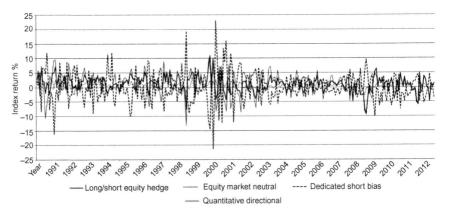

Figure 3.12 Historical performance of noninvestable HFRI long/short equity, equity market neutral, dedicated short bias, and quantitative directional indices

Fund Weighted Composite and Fund of Funds Composite indices are highly correlated, with a correlation coefficient of 0.87.

The indices that belong to the event-driven category also seem to be moving in tandem with each other in Figure 3.11, and the correlations between these three indices vary between 0.57 and 0.86. It is worth pointing out that the merger/risk arbitrage index moves in a narrower band and it was able to come out of the 2008 crisis relatively unscathed. Figures 3.12 and 3.13 display performance graphs for the

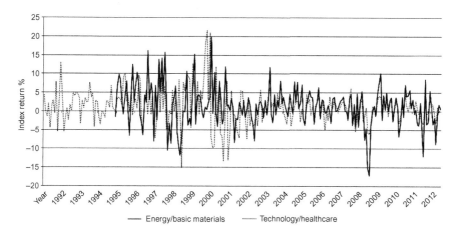

Figure 3.13 Historical performance of noninvestable HFRI energy/basic materials and technology/healthcare indices

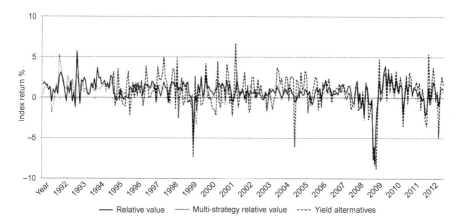

Figure 3.14 Historical performance of noninvestable HFRI relative value, multistrategy value, and yield alternatives indices

equity hedge category. We see that all indices in this category are highly volatile, with the largest swings belonging to the dedicated short bias index. An exception is the equity market neutral index, which also displays low absolute correlations with the other indices in its category. The dedicated short bias index has negative correlations with the other three indices in Figure 3.12, with pairwise correlation coefficients between -0.85 and -0.74. The correlation between the long/short equity hedge and quantitative directional indices is 0.89.

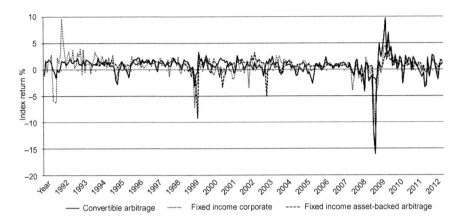

Figure 3.15 Historical performance of noninvestable HFRI convertible arbitrage, fixed-income corporate arbitrage, and fixed-income asset-backed arbitrage indices

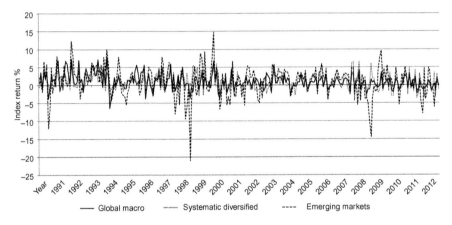

Figure 3.16 Historical performance of noninvestable HFRI global macro, systematic diversified, and emerging markets indices

The indices categorized as relative value are presented in Figures 3.14 and 3.15. The yield alternatives index seems to have experienced an extra shock in 2004, and it is also more volatile compared to the other indices in its category. The fixed-income asset-backed arbitrage strategy had mild losses during the 2008 crisis, whereas the other relative value substrategies experienced drastic drops in value exceeding 10%. The correlation of the returns of the fixed-income asset-backed arbitrage strategy with those of the other relative value substrategies is also much lower compared to the correlation coefficient between the corporate arbitrage and the convertible arbitrage indices, which is equal to 0.75. Finally, Figure 3.16 shows that the emerging markets index had larger swings compared to the global macro and systematic diversified indices, and it was especially hit during the LTCM meltdown in 1998. The correlations between these three indices range from 0.41 to 0.58.

Table 3.6 presents the descriptive statistics for the returns of the investable HFRX indices. Panel A presents statistics for the recent sample beginning from January 2005. We also have a small set of investable indices for which data is available from as early as December 1998. Descriptive statistics for this longer history of investable indices is presented in Panel B.

In Panel A, we see that there are four different investable composite indices compiled by HFR. These composite indices differ among themselves based on their scope of eligible funds and their correlation with traditional market benchmarks. The mean returns of all investable composite indices are low and vary between -0.079% and 0.035% per month. The lowest mean return belongs to the HFRX Absolute Return Index, whereas the highest mean return belongs to the HFRX Market Directional Index.

In the event-driven category, two indices with no noninvestable counterparts, namely the activist and credit arbitrage indices, performed strongly with average returns of 0.611% and 0.624%, respectively. Although the merger/risk arbitrage strategy was one of the poorly performing strategies in the earlier tables, its investable index compiled by HFR produces a relatively high average return of 0.380%. Distressed restructuring index has the weakest performance among the event-driven category with an average return of only -0.249%. In the event-driven category, the multistrategy event-driven strategy, which is able to switch opportunistically between event-driven strategies based on the market outlook, also performs well with an average return of 0.550%. In the equity hedge category, the best performers are the sector-oriented indices with 0.527% and 0.439% average returns for the technology/healthcare and energy/basic materials indices, respectively. The fundamental growth index also performs well with a mean return of 0.456% in contrast to the fundamental value index which has a negative mean return. The long/short equity hedge, equity market neutral, and dedicated short bias indices also have negative average returns with the dedicated short bias index being the worst performer with a mean return of −0.343%. In contrast, the quantitative directional has a decent average performance with a mean return of 0.375%.

There is some heterogeneity among the relative value category. The convertible arbitrage index has a low mean return of −0.296%, whereas the fixed income asset-backed index has a high mean return of 0.922%. The fixed income corporate arbitrage and fixed income sovereign arbitrage indices fall somewhere in between. The yield alternatives strategy, and especially its energy infrastructure substrategy, also display favorable performances with mean returns of 0.641% and 0.885%, respectively. The opportunistic multistrategy relative value index has an average return of 0.657%. When we turn to the global macro category, we see that the global macro index itself has a weak performance although many of its substrategies display favorable returns. For example, despite the contrast between their trading philosophies, the discretionary thematic and systematic diversified indices generate relatively high average returns of 0.621% and 0.554%, respectively. The currency index has a low mean return of 0.015%; however, the commodity index and especially its metals substrategy display strong performances with the latter generating a mean return of 1.361%. The emerging markets index is again a strong performer with a mean return of 0.911%.

The investable strategy indices in Table 3.6 do not match one-to-one with the noninvestable strategy indices in Table 3.5. However, for the indices we are able to compare, we observe that most of the investable indices have lower average returns compared to the noninvestable indices. This result is identical to the results from the DJCS database.

The investable HFRX composite indices all exhibit higher median returns compared to the mean returns. For the strategy indices, this finding generally holds with the major exception being the global macro category. Five out of ten indices under this category have mean returns that exceed the median returns. Outside the global macro category, with the exception of the credit arbitrage and quantitative directional indices, all strategies bear negatively skewed index returns. The most pronounced negative skewness is witnessed for the relative value category. The convertible arbitrage, fixed-income sovereign arbitrage, and fixed-income corporate arbitrage indices have skewness statistics that range between -5.212 and -3.355. The most positive skewness statistics are equal to 0.895 and 0.668 and belong to the agriculture and commodity indices, respectively. All investable composite HFRX indices are also negatively skewed with skewness statistics between -2.767 and -1.212.

The least volatile composite index is the HFRX Absolute Return Index with a standard deviation of 1.050% and the most volatile composite index is the HFRX Market Directional Index with a standard deviation of 2.957%. This is hardly surprising given that HFR discriminates between these two composite indices based on the volatilities of their constituent funds. Among the strategy indices, there are certain categories that stick out with their high volatilities. In the event-driven category, the activist and multistrategy event-driven indices are especially volatile with standard deviations of 4.532% and 3.014%, respectively. In contrast, the merger/risk arbitrage exhibits low volatility with a standard deviation of 1.009%. In the equity hedge category, equity market neutral index also has a low standard deviation of 1.184%; however, other indices in this category such as energy/basic materials, multistrategy equity hedge, and dedicated short bias have standard deviations between 3.718% and 4.020%. In the relative value category, the convertible arbitrage index sticks out as being highly volatile with a standard deviation of 4.578%. The yield alternatives index and its substrategy indices are also relatively volatile. Finally, the indices under the global macro category have mild volatilities with the exception of the metals and energy indices.

The comparison of the minimum and maximum index returns mirror the comparison of the median and mean returns. Although most indices display minimum returns whose absolute values exceed the mean returns, various indices under the global macro category violate this rule. We have already seen that some of these indices exhibit positive skewness. The most negative monthly return is equal to -34.683% and witnessed for the convertible arbitrage index. Other strategies that encountered large negative monthly shocks include the activist, energy, metals, and energy/basic materials strategies. These are also the strategies for which the indices also experienced the highest maximum returns. Again, all indices have some degree of leptokurtosis, and the largest kurtosis values are witnessed under the relative value category. The kurtosis statistics vary between 20.325 and 37.592 for the convertible arbitrage, fixed-income sovereign arbitrage, and fixed-income corporate arbitrage indices. Also, there is one highly leptokurtic investable composite index, which is the HFRX Equal Weighted Strategy Index with a kurtosis value of 15.398.

Panel B of Table 3.6 presents results for a handful of investable indices for which performance data extends back to 1998. First, we see that the mean returns have been lower in the recent period. For example, the return of the HFRX Global Hedge Fund Index is 0.458% in the full sample period, whereas it is only 0.017% in the recent sample period. Second, the median returns are again higher than the mean returns with the exception of the global macro index. Third, consequently, all indices except the global macro index exhibit negative skewness. Fourth, there is no significant difference in index volatilities between the two sample periods. Finally, we again see substantial leptokurtosis in index returns in the full sample period and the kurtosis statistic for the convertible arbitrage strategy is as high as 65.763.

Figure 3.17 presents historical performances for HFRX composite indices. One can again see that the indices are prone to frequent up and down movements, and they have been very sensitive towards the two crisis periods in 1998 and 2008. The more recent financial crisis seems to

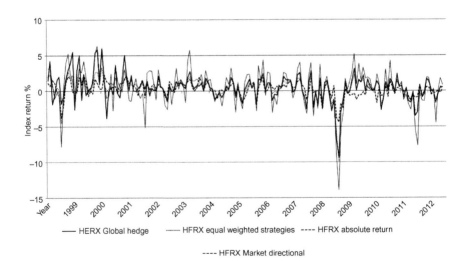

Figure 3.17 Historical performance of investable HFRX global hedge, equal-weighted strategies, absolute return, and market directional indices

have had a more adverse impact on the hedge fund industry. About 35% of the monthly returns have been negative for the HFRX composite indices over the full sample period. The correlations between the composite indices are high and vary between 0.61 and 0.80.

Figures 3.18 and 3.19 pertain to the event-driven category. We see that the distressed restructuring index was hit badly in 2008, whereas the merger/risk arbitrage index came out of the crisis relatively unscathed. The correlations between most event-driven indices are greater than 0.60, with the exception of merger/risk arbitrage, which

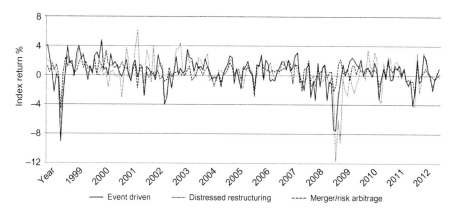

Figure 3.18 Historical performance of investable HFRX event-driven, distressed restructuring, and merger/risk arbitrage indices

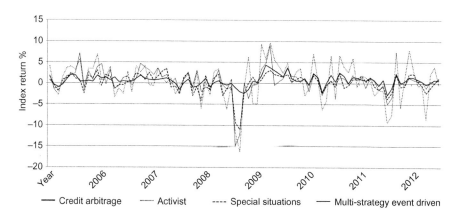

Figure 3.19 Historical performance of investable HFRX credit arbitrage, activist, special situations, and multi-strategy event-driven indices

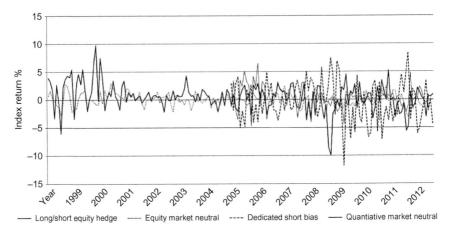

Figure 3.20 Historical performance of investable HFRX long/short equity hedge, equity market neutral, dedicated short bias, and quantitative market neutral indices

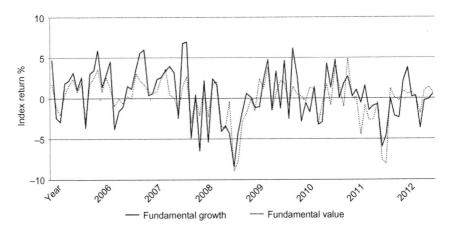

Figure 3.21 Historical performance of investable HFRX fundamental growth and fundamental value indices

seems to be less in tandem with the other strategies in the same category.

Figures 3.20–3.22 present performance graphs for the indices under the equity hedge category. In Figure 3.20, we can see that the dedicated short bias index moves in a wider band compared to other equity hedge indices, and the correlations between most of these indices is low, with the exception of long/short equity hedge and quantitative directional, which have a correlation coefficient of 0.55. In

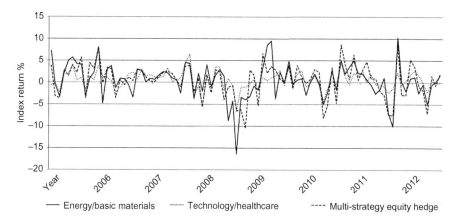

Figure 3.22 Historical performance of investable HFRX energy/basic materials, technology/healthcare, and multi-strategy equity hedge indices

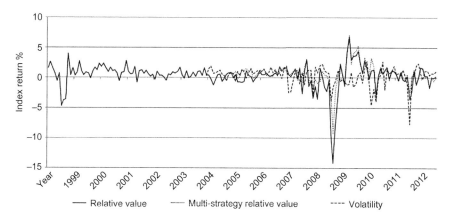

Figure 3.23 Historical performance of investable HFRX relative value, multistrategy relative value and volatility indices

Figure 3.21, we see that, although the mean return of the fundamental growth index was much higher compared to that of the fundamental value index, the two indices move in tandem with each other and their correlation coefficient is 0.77. The difference in the mean returns is due to the fact that the fundamental value index cannot hit the same peaks as the fundamental growth index even when it is ascending.

The indices under the relative value category are presented in Figures 3.23–3.25. It seems to be the case that the 2008 crisis hit this category particularly hard with the exception of the volatility index.

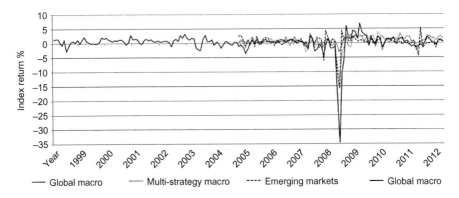

Figure 3.24 Historical performance of fixed-income convertible arbitrage, fixed-income corporate arbitrage, fixed-income sovereign arbitrage, and fixed-income asset-backed arbitrage indices

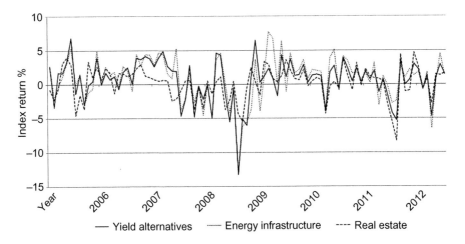

Figure 3.25 Historical performance of investable HFRX yield alternatives, energy infrastructure, and real estate indices

This index, by nature, benefits from tumultuous market conditions and, consequently, its correlation with the other relative value indices is low. As seen in Figure 3.24, the crisis also did not affect the returns of the fixed-income asset-backed strategy drastically, whereas its impact on the other arbitrage-based strategies in the fixed-income market was deep. Excluding the fixed-income asset-backed arbitrage strategy, the correlation coefficients between the other three indices in Figure 3.24 range between 0.69 and 0.89. The yield alternatives strategy and its substrategies in Figure 3.25 also have highly correlated

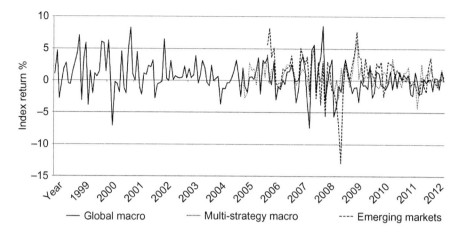

Figure 3.26 Historical performance of investable HFRX global macro, multistrategy global macro, and emerging markets indices

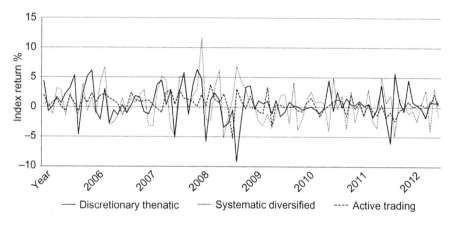

Figure 3.27 Historical performance of investable HFRX discretionary thematic, systematic diversified, and active trading indices

returns, although the real estate index moves in a narrower band and managed to protect itself from the 2008 crisis relative to the other indices.

Figure 3.26 presents the global macro and the emerging markets indices. The latter index was more volatile and was hit more adversely in 2008 than the former. Figure 3.27 presents three substrategies under the global macro category. The discretionary thematic and systematic diversified strategies are at the opposite ends of the spectrum regarding their investment thesis, and the active trading strategy is a hybrid of

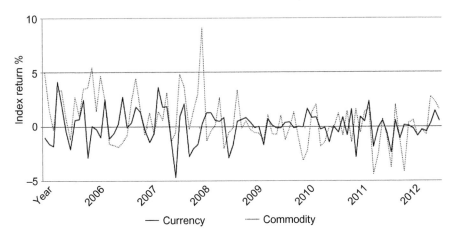

Figure 3.28 Historical performance of investable HFRX currency and commodity indices

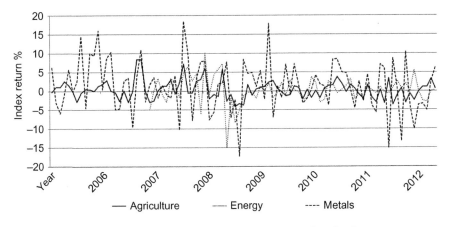

Figure 3.29 Historical performance of investable HFRX agriculture, energy, and metals indices

them. Consequently, the correlation of these three indices is relatively low with coefficients between 0.12 and 0.31. The currency and commodity indices depicted in Figure 3.28 have a correlation coefficient of only 0.26, with the commodity index hitting higher peaks and deeper troughs, especially beginning from 2008. These wild swings are even more pronounced for the metals index in Figure 3.29. The correlations between the three commodity substrategies are only between 0.16 and 0.37. One can also see that the agriculture index was able to absorb the negative shock during the credit crunch of 2008 better than the other commodity substrategies.

CHAPTER 4

Risk-Adjusted Performances of Hedge Fund Indices

The risks associated with the dynamic trading strategies adopted by hedge funds are manifold. First, there is the market risk or systematic risk that affects all financial securities and asset management companies. This is the risk associated with the movements in variables such as security prices, interest rates, and exchange rates that affect broad capital markets. A special feature of the hedge fund industry is that it is allowed to make heavy use of leverage, and this practice has the potential to magnify market risks. Bali et al. (2012) have investigated the extent to which market risk and residual risk explain the cross-sectional dispersion in hedge fund returns. They find that systematic risk is a highly significant factor explaining the dispersion of cross-sectional returns, whereas measures of residual risk have little explanatory power.

Second, there are the credit risks faced by a hedge fund. These risks are related to the operational structure and organizational processes of a hedge fund or its counterparties. For example, if one of the fund's counterparties goes bankrupt or a security in the portfolio of the fund loses significant value, such events create credit risks for the hedge fund. Third, there are the liquidity risks. As explained in Chapter 1, the liquidity risk of a hedge fund may originate from two sources. First, although many hedge fund investors are subject to lock up and similar restrictions, their redemption requests could cause liquidity problems for a hedge fund. Second, many hedge funds carry highly illiquid assets in their holdings which may cause an extra risk in relation to the values of their overall portfolios. These three major sources of risk impact different hedge fund indices in different ways. Long/short equity hedge funds are exposed to short squeeze risks, merger/risk arbitrage funds are subject to event risk, distressed restructuring funds are subject to credit and liquidity risks, emerging market funds are subject to sovereign risk, and so on.

Many hedge funds advertise themselves on the strength of their historical returns. A fund that generates higher returns than the average fund in its peer group prides itself for beating the competition. However, returns constitute only one dimension of performance. Although risk is equally important to returns, most funds do not spend enough effort to document how much risk they have undertaken in order to generate the returns they did. Can we clearly say that a fund with higher risk that generates a higher return performs better than a fund with lower risk that generates a lower return? The answer to this question is ambiguous because what really matters is the ability of a hedge fund to generate higher returns per unit risk. Without taking both return and risk into account, we would be comparing apples and oranges since the risks taken by hedge funds and funds' underlying strategies vary widely. Therefore, in this chapter, we calculate the risk-adjusted performances of various hedge fund strategies and compare them to each other. Doing so serves the purpose of giving diverse hedge fund indices an equal footing. Of course, this is easier said than done because there are many different possible risk measures, and it is possible that hedge fund indices may rank differently based on which risk measure is used. Also, there is no conceptual cohesion between different risk measures. Our goals are to comment on various risk-adjusted performance measures, provide the logic behind each measure, and highlight their strengths and weaknesses.

4.1 SHARPE RATIO

The Sharpe ratio is one of the most popular reward-to-risk ratios in both the academia and the industry. It is equal to the return of a hedge fund above the risk-free rate scaled by the fund's return volatility as measured by standard deviation. We calculate a Sharpe ratio for each hedge fund index i for each month t using the following formula:

$$\text{Sharpe ratio}_{i,t} = \frac{R_{i,t} - R_{f,t}}{\sigma_t} \tag{4.1}$$

where $R_{i,t}$ denotes the average return of the hedge fund index i during the last 36 months and $R_{f,t}$ denotes the risk-free rate at the end of month t. We calculate the standard deviation in the denominator, σ_t, as the standard deviation of the monthly index returns over the past 36 months. A greater Sharpe ratio implies that the hedge fund index has generated a higher excess return per unit of risk. An advantage of the Sharpe ratio is that it is not affected by the leverage that a hedge fund undertakes.

Tables 4.1–4.4 present the Sharpe ratios for all the hedge fund indices considered in our empirical analyses. Tables 4.1 and 4.2 present the results for the DJCS noninvestable and investable indices, respectively. Tables 4.3 and 4.4 present the results for the HFR noninvestable and investable indices, respectively. To calculate the Sharpe ratios, we need 36 months of historical data; therefore, the monthly series for the Sharpe ratios for each index begins exactly 36 months after the return series. We again report full sample and recent sample results for the noninvestable indices in order to both observe the historical change in the Sharpe ratios and compare investable and noninvestable indices during a common time window. For example, the recent period in Tables 4.1 and 4.2 begins on October 2007 and the recent period in Tables 4.3 and 4.4 begins on January 2008. This time window is also interesting due to the fact that it corresponds to the post-crisis period after the recent credit crunch. This timing convention also applies to all the risk-adjusted performance metrics that we will introduce later.

Remember that we calculate a Sharpe ratio for each month and hedge fund index following Eq. (4.1). The tables report the arithmetic averages of these monthly Sharpe ratios. Most empirical studies calculate a single Sharpe ratio for the sample periods under consideration; however, doing so assumes that the risk-to-reward ratio for an index is constant over time. As we will later see, the Sharpe ratios are time-varying, and we aim to capture this time variation by adopting a methodology that constructs the ratios in a rolling window fashion.

In Table 4.1, we see that the highest Sharpe ratio is 0.598, and it belongs to the equity market neutral index. The interpretation of this number is that the equity market neutral index generates almost 60 basis points of excess returns per unit of standard deviation, on average. This is worth scrutiny because the equity market neutral index has

Table 4.1 Sharpe Ratios for DJCS Noninvestable Hedge Fund Indices

	Full Sample	Recent Sample
Event driven	0.44795	0.23859
Distressed restructuring	0.47057	0.21381
Merger/risk arbitrage	0.28929	0.31081
Multistrategy event driven	0.38173	0.24519
Long/short equity hedge	0.25390	0.15427
Equity market neutral	0.59795	0.16415
Dedicated short bias	− 0.08716	− 0.06529
Convertible arbitrage	0.34980	0.10638
Fixed-income arbitrage	0.28265	0.04721
Global macro	0.45858	0.38262
Emerging markets	0.21036	0.17198
Managed futures	0.09826	0.15690
Multistrategy	0.42675	0.18235
DJCS Hedge Fund Index	0.32384	0.19946
S&P 500 Index	0.09334	− 0.02468

Table 4.2 Sharpe Ratios for DJCS Investable Hedge Fund Indices

	Recent Sample
Event driven	0.15085
Long/short equity hedge	0.00880
Equity market neutral	− 0.08357
Dedicated short bias	− 0.07991
Convertible arbitrage	− 0.00319
Fixed-income arbitrage	− 0.14612
Global macro	0.04011
Emerging markets	0.05673
Managed futures	0.17919
Multistrategy	0.02270
DJCS AllHedge Index	0.04940
S&P 500 Index	− 0.02942

the second to last mean return in Table 3.1. However, it also has a lower than average standard deviation, and with this risk adjustment, the index experiences a drastic improvement in its comparative performance. This finding alone is sufficient to conclude that adjusting for

Table 4.3 Sharpe Ratios for HFR Noninvestable Hedge Fund Indices

	Full Sample	Recent Sample
Event driven	0.46593	0.12535
Distressed restructuring	0.51183	0.11286
Merger/risk arbitrage	0.53267	0.33334
Long/short equity hedge	0.35819	0.06511
Equity market neutral	0.36760	0.08648
Quantitative directional	0.25269	0.05383
Dedicated short bias	− 0.04137	0.00816
Energy/basic materials	0.24559	0.07895
Technology/health care	0.23728	0.19772
Relative value	0.61646	0.24928
Convertible arbitrage	0.49855	0.11094
Fixed-income corporate arbitrage	0.33842	0.05801
Fixed-income asset-backed arbitrage	0.72469	0.47562
Yield alternatives	0.22484	0.04846
Multistrategy relative value	0.56608	0.10830
Global macro	0.36124	0.32056
Systematic diversified	0.34112	0.28698
Emerging markets	0.28757	0.13301
Fund of funds composite	0.26494	0.02687
Fund of funds conservative	0.33908	0.01140
Fund of funds diversified	0.22763	0.02776
Fund of funds market defensive	0.26690	0.27673
Fund of funds strategic	0.24539	0.02091
HFRI Fund Weighted Composite Index	0.41357	0.13899
S&P 500 Index	0.11072	− 0.04188

risk is essential to obtain a meaningful comparison of index performance. After the equity market neutral index, the indices with the highest volatility adjusted returns are the distressed restructuring, global macro, and event-driven indices with Sharpe ratios between 0.471 and 0.448. These three indices are also among the top four based on their mean returns. Ignoring the equity market neutral index, the other two equity hedge indices have weak volatility adjusted performances. It is not a surprise that the dedicated short bias strategy ranks at the bottom with its Sharpe ratio of −0.087 because this index also had the lowest mean return. However, the long/short equity hedge

Table 4.4 Sharpe Ratios for HFR Investable Hedge Fund Indices		
	Recent Sample	**Full Sample**
Event driven	− 0.01263	0.19322
Distressed restructuring	− 0.19866	0.14389
Merger/risk arbitrage	0.38567	0.29759
Credit arbitrage	0.39908	−
Activist	0.08809	−
Special situations	− 0.00151	−
Multistrategy event driven	0.13884	−
Long/short equity hedge	− 0.07107	0.17038
Equity market neutral	− 0.03707	−0.04679
Quantitative directional	0.02832	−
Dedicated short bias	− 0.00810	−
Fundamental growth	0.09388	−
Fundamental value	− 0.03351	−
Energy/basic materials	0.06306	−
Technology/health care	0.20452	−
Multistrategy equity hedge	0.11654	−
Relative value	− 0.01755	0.27901
Convertible arbitrage	− 0.11426	0.17690
Fixed-income corporate arbitrage	0.07352	−
Fixed-income sovereign arbitrage	0.09257	−
Fixed-income asset-backed arbitrage	0.62115	−
Yield alternatives	0.12377	−
Energy infrastructure	0.17266	−
Real estate	0.00949	−
Volatility	0.07651	0.12552
Multistrategy relative value	0.31949	−
Global macro	0.00701	0.15204
Discretionary thematic	0.15236	−
Systematic diversified	0.22068	−
Active trading	0.40899	−
Currency	0.00540	−
Commodity	0.23492	−
Agriculture	0.14885	−
Energy	− 0.00474	−
Metals	0.23795	−
Multistrategy global macro	0.28933	−

(Continued)

Table 4.4 (Continued)		
	Recent Sample	Full Sample
Emerging markets	0.20644	–
HFRX Global Hedge Fund Index	– 0.04223	0.20027
HFRX Equal Weighted Strategies Index	– 0.04049	0.27545
HFRX Absolute Return Index	– 0.16983	0.19473
HFRX Market Directional Index	0.01130	0.18111
S&P 500 Index	– 0.04188	−0.00200

index which is in the top three based on mean returns ranks only the tenth based on Sharpe ratios. This finding again attests to the importance of adjusting for risk. The other two indices that have the lowest Sharpe ratios are the emerging markets and managed futures indices. These strategies rank somewhere in the middle for average returns, but they have the highest standard deviations after the dedicated short bias strategy. Consequently, their relatively high volatilities push the two strategies to the bottom of the rankings based on Sharpe ratios. The two indices under the relative value category, namely, convertible arbitrage and fixed-income arbitrage, are poor to mediocre performers based on their mean returns, and they continue to be so based on Sharpe ratios.

The composite DJCS Hedge Fund Index would have ranked eighth among the strategy indices with its Sharpe ratio of 0.324. We also report volatility adjusted performances for the S&P 500 Index. This is an equity index which covers the largest 500 firms in the USA, and it is commonly used as a performance benchmark for traditional asset classes. However, since hedge funds have dynamic trading strategies, use leverage, and frequently invest in assets that are outside the scope of S&P 500, the S&P 500 Index is not the most appropriate benchmark as far as our hedge fund indices are concerned. We report volatility adjusted performance statistics for the S&P 500 Index in order to see whether hedge funds can provide superior returns compared to a traditional equity index through their absolute return focus. We find that this is indeed the case. The S&P 500 Index has a Sharpe ratio of 0.093 during the full sample period. This figure corresponds to less than a third of the Sharpe ratio of the DJCS Hedge Fund Index. Moreover, the S&P 500 Index can only beat the dedicated short bias strategy, and it provides an inferior volatility adjusted performance compared to all other hedge fund indices.

In the recent sample, we observe that only three indices increase their volatility-adjusted performances. These indices belong to the merger/risk arbitrage, managed futures, and dedicated short bias strategies. The magnitudes of these increases are small. For the other hedge fund indices, we observe substantial drops in the Sharpe ratios. The equity market neutral index experiences a particularly sharp decrease in its Sharpe ratio from 0.598 to 0.164. As a result, it is no longer the top performing hedge fund strategy and slips down to the eighth rank. This observation is not surprising because, in Table 3.2, the equity market neutral has the second lowest mean return and the second highest standard deviation. The other two indices in the equity hedge category also continue to be weak volatility adjusted performers. The highest Sharpe ratio in the recent sample period belongs to the global macro index and is equal to 0.383. The global macro index has the highest mean return and the second lowest standard deviation in Table 3.2. The other category that has a strong volatility adjusted performance is the event-driven category. The four indices in this category follow the global macro index with Sharpe ratios varying between 0.214 and 0.311. The index that deserves the most attention in this group is the merger/risk arbitrage index. Despite its low average return, the merger/risk arbitrage index has the lowest standard deviation in Table 3.2, and this low volatility pays off by granting the index the second highest Sharpe ratio in the recent period after the global macro strategy. The convertible arbitrage and fixed income arbitrage indices have Sharpe ratios of 0.106 and 0.047, respectively, and they are the worst volatility adjusted performers after the dedicated short bias strategy. Emerging markets and managed futures indices surpass these two relative value indices in the recent period, but their respective Sharpe ratios of 0.172 and 0.157 still place them in the bottom half of the rankings. DJCS Hedge Fund Index also experiences a drop in its Sharpe ratio from 0.324 to 0.199, and it would rank the sixth among the strategy indices. S&P 500 Index has a negative average Sharpe ratio in the recent sample period and is only able to beat the dedicated short bias index.

Table 4.2 presents the Sharpe ratios of the investable DJCS hedge fund indices. First of all, the Sharpe ratios of all strategies, except that of managed futures, are lower for the investable indices compared to their noninvestable counterparts. We already observed that investable indices had lower mean returns compared to noninvestable indices in Table 3.3

and now, we find that this also translates to the volatility-adjusted performances. The highest Sharpe ratio belongs to the managed futures strategy and is equal to 0.179. Considering that the noninvestable managed futures index was a weak performer, we can conclude that the investable managed futures funds are way better performers with respect to the noninvestable managed futures funds. The event-driven index is also strong with its Sharpe ratio of 0.151. Two directional strategies, emerging markets and global macro, come next with their Sharpe ratios of 0.057 and 0.040. It is worthwhile to emphasize once more that these figures are much lower than the Sharpe ratios of the noninvestable indices for the same strategies. The indices under the equity hedge category rank at the bottom half, and two of these indices, namely, equity market neutral and dedicated short bias, have negative average Sharpe ratios. The convertible arbitrage and fixed income arbitrage indices also have negative Sharpe ratios. The convertible arbitrage index has a positive mean return in Table 3.3; therefore, its negative Sharpe ratio indicates that the positive returns occurred in periods of comparatively higher volatility. The Sharpe ratio for the investable DJCS AllHedge Index is equal to 0.049 and is about a quarter of the Sharpe ratio of the noninvestable DJCS Hedge Fund Index during the recent sample period. Nevertheless, DJCS AllHedge Index would have ranked the fourth among the investable strategy indices. Finally, the S&P 500 Index has a negative average Sharpe ratio of −0.029 in the recent sample period and lags behind 7 out of 10 strategy indices.

Next, we investigate the noninvestable and investable indices provided by HFR. Our goal again is not comparing the numbers between the DJCS and HFR databases, but we want to explore whether the general patterns observed in DJCS are also encountered in HFR. Table 4.3 presents the full sample results for noninvestable HFR hedge fund indices. One should also remember that the data availability in HFR extends to four years earlier than that for DJCS, so the full sample results in Tables 4.1 and 4.3 are also not comparable based on the sample periods aside from the different methodologies used by the two databases. The noninvestable HFRI Fund Weighted Composite Index has a Sharpe ratio of 0.414, whereas the S&P 500 Index has a Sharpe ratio of 0.111. The volatility adjusted performance of the S&P 500 Index is worse than all composite fund of funds indices and all strategy indices with the exception of dedicated short bias. This is another manifestation of the conjecture that investing in hedge funds is more profitable in volatility adjusted terms than investing in a common equity index. In other words, hedge funds seem to be generating alpha above and beyond the equity market.

Looking at the different strategy categories, we observe that two main groups stick out with their strong volatility adjusted performances. The first of these categories is relative value. The highest Sharpe ratio among all strategy indices belongs to fixed income asset-backed arbitrage. Table 3.4 shows that this index ranks in the middle based on its mean return, but its standard deviation is among the lowest ones. This comparatively low volatility rewards the index with the highest Sharpe ratio again highlighting the importance of adjusting for risk while assessing performance. The relative value and multistrategy relative value indices also have high Sharpe ratios of 0.616 and 0.566, along with the convertible arbitrage index, which ranks in the top third. On the other hand, fixed-income corporate arbitrage and yield alternatives indices have Sharpe ratios below that of the HFRI Fund Weighted Composite Index due to their average standard deviations but low mean returns. The other category that sticks out is the event-driven category, and the three indices here all outperform the HFRI Fund Weighted Composite Index. The index with the best volatility-adjusted performance in this category is the merger/risk arbitrage index with a Sharpe ratio of 0.533.

The equity hedge category continues to be a weak performer based on Sharpe ratios. Table 3.4 shows that four of the indices in this category are among the five indices with the highest mean returns. However, four of the five indices with the highest standard deviations are also in this category. Accordingly, when we rank all the strategy indices based on their Sharpe ratios, we find that four of the worst performers are under the equity hedge category. In other words, the high average returns of these indices are not enough to compensate for their high volatilities. The worst volatility adjusted equity hedge index is dedicated short bias with a Sharpe ratio of -0.041 and the best volatility adjusted equity hedge index is equity market neutral with a Sharpe ratio of 0.368, which is still lower than that of the composite noninvestable HFR index. The equity market neutral index has the second lowest mean return but also the lowest standard deviation and, as a result, its Sharpe ratio is higher than the other indices in its category.

The global macro and systematic diversified indices rank somewhere in the middle, whereas the emerging markets index lags behind and ranks the thirteenth. The latter index has one of the top three average returns; however, its comparatively high standard deviations hurt its Sharpe ratio. Finally, all the funds of hedge funds indices have Sharpe ratios that are below that of the HFRI Fund Weighted Composite Index. The lowest Sharpe ratio of 0.228 belongs to the diversified fund of funds strategy and the highest Sharpe ratio of 0.339 belongs to the conservative fund of funds strategy. All the fund of funds indices would rank at the bottom half if we were to include them among the strategy indices.

When we focus on the recent sample period, we observe that the only two indices that have a higher Sharpe ratio compared to the full sample period are the dedicated short bias and market defensive fund of funds indices. Both of these indices are defined by the short exposures underlying their corresponding strategies. Thus, it is no wonder why these two indices improved their performance in a period which is marked by significant equity market declines. Despite the increase in its Sharpe ratio, the dedicated short bias index is still the strategy index with the worst volatility-adjusted performance. On the other hand, the market defensive fund of funds index is the best performer among the five fund of funds indices. The Sharpe ratio of the market defensive fund of funds index is equal to 0.277, whereas the Sharpe ratios of the other fund of funds indices vary between only 0.011 and 0.028. The market defensive fund of funds index also comfortably beats the HFRI Fund Weighted Composite Index which has a Sharpe ratio of 0.139. The S&P 500 Index again has a negative average Sharpe ratio and ranks behind all strategy indices.

The fixed-income asset-backed arbitrage and merger/risk arbitrage indices have Sharpe ratios of 0.476 and 0.333, respectively, and are still among the top-performing strategy indices. One notable difference is related to the global macro and systematic diversified indices which rank in the bottom half during the full sample period. During the recent years, the global macro index moves up to the third rank due to its comparatively low standard deviation, and the systematic diversified index moves up to the fourth rank due to its comparatively high mean return. The equity hedge category again continues poorly, and five of the six indices in this category constitute the bottom tercile among the strategy indices. The only exception is the technology/health care index with a Sharpe ratio of 0.198, thanks to the strategy's high mean return. The indices under the relative value category are the top volatility adjusted performers over the full sample; however, they slip down the rankings during the recent sample period. The yield alternatives and the convertible arbitrage indices are at the bottom of the list with Sharpe ratios of only 0.048 and 0.058. The only strong performer in this category remains the fixed-income asset-backed arbitrage index which has a Sharpe ratio of 0.476. Finally, the emerging markets index improves its position in the rankings due to the fact that it is the index with the third-highest mean return in the recent sample period. However, the emerging markets index also has the second highest standard deviation, and it is able to climb up to only the seventh position in the Sharpe ratio rankings.

Table 4.4 presents the Sharpe ratios for the HFRX investable indices. We begin our discussion from the recent sample period. First of all, we observe that most of the investable indices once again have lower Sharpe ratios compared to the corresponding noninvestable indices. However, there are notable exceptions to this pattern, and four of these exceptions are grouped under the relative value category. We can conclude that investable hedge funds that followed fixed-income corporate arbitrage, fixed-income asset-backed arbitrage, yield alternatives, and multistrategy relative value strategies outperformed their noninvestable counterparts during the recent sample period on a volatility-adjusted basis. The other strategies outside the relative value category that exhibit the same property are merger/risk arbitrage, technology/health care, and emerging markets.

We also find that three of the composite indices have negative Sharpe ratios in the recent sample period except the HFRX Market Directional Index which has a Sharpe ratio of 0.011. This is also the only composite index that can clearly outperform the S&P 500 Index. This result is new and attests to the conjecture that investable hedge funds did not have an overwhelming tendency to generate volatility adjusted returns above and beyond what a traditional equity market was able to achieve.

We will discuss the results category by category, but we also need to point out that each category embeds a large amount of heterogeneity in itself. In the event-driven category, the indices that stand out the most are the credit arbitrage and merger/risk arbitrage indices with their Sharpe ratios of 0.399 and 0.386, respectively. These two indices do not have stellar mean returns in Table 3.6; however, they are among the indices with the lowest standard deviations. The worst performers in the event-driven category are the distressed restructuring, event-driven, and special situations indices with their Sharpe ratios that range from −0.199 to −0.002. The equity hedge category is the only category that performs weakly across the board. Except the technology/health care index which ranks eleventh with a Sharpe ratio of 0.205, all the indices in the equity hedge category belong to the bottom half of the investable index Sharpe ratio rankings. Again, this finding does not come as a surprise since many indices in this category such as the long/short equity hedge, equity market neutral, dedicated short bias, and fundamental value indices have negative average returns in the recent sample period.

There is a wide dispersion in Sharpe ratios for the relative value category. The index with the highest volatility-adjusted performance, the fixed-income asset-backed arbitrage index, belongs to this category with a Sharpe ratio of 0.621. This index has one of the highest three mean returns and lowest three standard deviations in Table 3.6. The opportunistic multistrategy relative value index ranks fifth with a Sharpe ratio of 0.319. Other than this, all the hedge fund indices under the relative value category have mediocre or poor volatility adjusted performances. The convertible arbitrage index has the second-lowest mean return and the second-highest standard deviation in Table 3.6; thus, this index has the lowest Sharpe ratio in its category.

The global macro category is also heterogenous. The active trading index has the second highest volatility adjusted performance among all HFRX indices with a Sharpe ratio of 0.409. This strategy is a mixture of the discretionary thematic and systematic diversified strategies, and it has a lower mean return than both in Table 3.6. However, the active trading strategy also has one of the lowest standard deviations, and this low volatility pays off in the form of a relatively high Sharpe ratio. The multistrategy global macro and commodity indices also rank in the top quartile among the other strategy indices with their Sharpe ratios of 0.289 and 0.235, respectively. A curious case is the metals index because this index has both the highest average return and the highest standard deviation in Table 3.6. As a result, we observe that the metals index is still a relatively strong performer, but it drops down to the seventh position based on its Sharpe ratio of 0.238. The currency and energy indices in the global macro category are close to the bottom of the rankings with their Sharpe ratios of 0.005 and −0.005, respectively. Finally, the emerging markets index which has the third highest mean return in Table 3.6 drops down to the tenth place in Sharpe ratio rankings due to its relatively higher standard deviation.

A handful of investable HFRX indices also have data that go back to 1998. Table 4.4 shows that the only index that substantially improves its volatility adjusted performance in the recent sample period is the merger/risk arbitrage index. Still, this index has a Sharpe ratio of 0.298 which is the highest one during the full sample period. The relative value index follows the merger/risk arbitrage index with a Sharpe ratio of 0.279. The worst volatility-adjusted performers during the full sample are the volatility and distressed restructuring investable indices with Sharpe ratios of 0.126 and 0.144, respectively. The composite investable indices also have higher Sharpe ratios for the full sample period compared to the recent sample period. The Sharpe ratios of the composite indices vary between 0.181 for the HFRX Market Directional Index and 0.275 for the HFRX Equal Weighted Strategies Index.

Finally, we present figures that capture how the historical volatility adjusted performances of various hedge fund indices have evolved through time. In Chapter 3, we were able to present the historical return graphs for all indices in both databases, but this is infeasible for the risk-adjusted returns because risk is defined in alternative ways in this chapter. As a result, we select the major composite and strategy indices and focus on the HFR database to give a general idea regarding the historical performance of the hedge fund industry.

Figure 4.1 presents Sharpe ratios for the noninvestable HFRI Fund Weighted Composite Index, Fund of Funds Composite Index, and S&P 500 Index. We observe that, although there are some short periods of time during which the S&P 500 Index generates a better volatility-adjusted performance than the composite hedge fund indices, the curve for the S&P Index generally lies below those of the other indices. The Sharpe ratios of the hedge fund indices are especially high during the early 1990s, after which we observe a recognizable downward trend. The correlation coefficient between the Sharpe ratios of

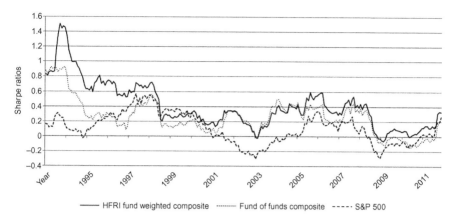

Figure 4.1 Sharpe ratios for HFRI fund weighted composite, fund of funds composite, and S&P 500 indices

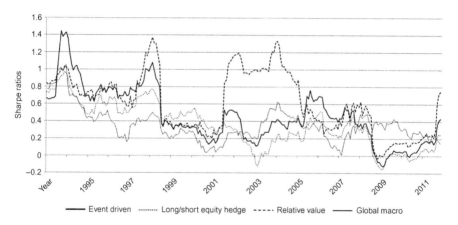

Figure 4.2 Sharpe ratios for HFRI event driven, long/short equity hedge, relative value, and global macro indices

the HFRI Fund Weighted Composite Index and Fund of Funds Composite Index is equal to 0.86, whereas the pairwise correlations with the S&P 500 Index are much lower. Figure 4.2 presents Sharpe ratios for the major noninvestable strategy indices. The event-driven index experiences a peak during the early 1990s, whereas the long/short equity hedge index generates a strong volatility adjusted performance between 2002 and 2005. There is a sharp decline in the Sharpe ratios of all indices except that of the global macro index during the 2008 financial crisis; however, these indices bounced back since then. The correlation coefficient between the event-driven and long/short equity hedge index is equal to 0.90, and the other pairwise correlations are between 0.43 and 0.59.

Figure 4.3 presents Sharpe ratios for the investable HFRX Global Hedge Fund Index, Equal Weighted Strategies Index, and S&P 500 Index. Again, the downward trend in the composite hedge fund indices is evident. The hedge fund indices dominated the S&P 500 Index during the first half of the 2000s, but the comparative performances have been close since then. The S&P 500 Index has a negative correlation with the composite hedge fund indices particularly due to the initial years of the sample period. The HFRX Global Hedge Fund Index and the Equal Weighted Strategies Index have a correlation coefficient of 0.94. Figure 4.4 presents Sharpe ratios for the major investable strategy indices. This figure looks very much like Figure 4.2

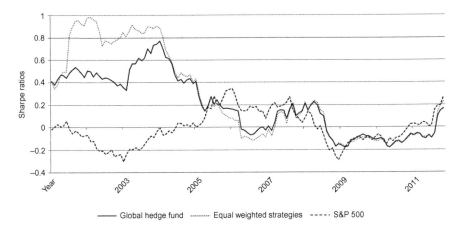

Figure 4.3 Sharpe ratios for HFRX global hedge fund, equal-weighted strategies, and S&P 500 indices

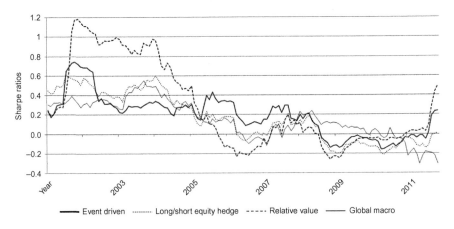

Figure 4.4 Sharpe ratios for HFRX event driven, long/short equity hedge, relative value, and global macro indices

with the long/short equity index dominating between 2002 and 2005 and a subsequent convergence in Sharpe ratios. The global macro index was able to survive the 2008 crisis without much damage, whereas the other indices experienced large Sharpe ratio declines and subsequent comebacks. The correlation coefficient between the relative value and long/short equity hedge index is equal to 0.86, and the other pairwise correlations are between 0.60 and 0.85.

4.2 SORTINO RATIO

As explained in Chapter 3, the standard deviation is an incomplete measure of risk because it ignores the non-normality of hedge fund returns and does not discriminate between favorable and unfavorable returns. We have seen that most hedge fund index distributions are negatively skewed and highly leptokurtic. Under these conditions, the standard deviation may not be able to capture all relevant dimensions of investing in hedge funds. We have already seen that hedge fund indices tend to display extreme returns that cannot be justified by a normal distribution, and these extreme returns are generally more pronounced for the left tail of fund index return distributions. Fung and Hsieh (2001) focus on trend-following hedge fund strategies, and Mitchell and Pulvino (2001) investigate risk arbitrageurs to find that nonlinear option-like payoffs are an integral feature of the payoffs of hedge fund strategies. Agarwal and Naik (2004) extend the hedge fund universe used in these two studies and argue that a large number of equity oriented hedge fund strategies exhibit payoffs resembling a short position on a put option on the market index and also bear significant left-tail risk. Therefore, ignoring the tail risk of hedge funds can result in significantly higher losses during large market downturns. To take this type of tail risk into account, we turn to the concept of downside risk. A couple of studies confirm the importance of downside risk in hedge fund performance assessment. Bali et al. (2007) conduct portfolio and regression analysis to find that there is a significantly positive relation between downside risk and the cross section of expected returns on hedge funds even after controlling for factors such as fund size and liquidity. Liang and Park (2010) find that common downside risk measures are superior to standard deviation in terms of predicting hedge fund failures.

In a recent paper by Bali et al. (2013), it is indicated that hedge funds' extensive use of derivatives, short-selling, and leverage and their dynamic trading strategies create significant non-normalities in their return distributions. Hence, the traditional performance measures fail to provide an accurate characterization of the relative strength of hedge fund portfolios. Bali et al. (2013) use alternative performance measures to determine which hedge fund strategies outperform the US equity and/or bond markets. Their results show that the long/short equity hedge and emerging markets hedge fund strategies outperform the US equity market, and the long/short equity hedge, multistrategy, managed futures, and global macro hedge fund strategies dominate the US treasury market.

The first ratio that we use to reflect downside risk is the Sortino ratio. The idea behind the Sortino ratio is that a significant component of risk is not volatility, but rather downside risk. The Sortino ratio is similar to the Sharpe ratio but replaces the risk-free rate in the Sharpe ratio with a possibly different minimum acceptable rate of return. More importantly, the volatility in the denominator is replaced by the semideviation of the return distribution around the specified minimum acceptable rate of return.

The calculation of semi-deviation is similar to that of standard deviation. The main difference is that semideviation only takes the deviations of observations that are lower than a benchmark into account. The choice of the benchmark is important and, for our analysis, we use the monthly risk-free rate in the USA as the benchmark. We calculate a semi-deviation for each hedge fund index i for each month t using the following formula:

$$\text{Semideviation}_{i,t} = \frac{1}{36} \sqrt{\sum_{\tau=t-36}^{t-1} d_{i,\tau}^2} \qquad (4.2)$$

where

$$d_{i,\tau} = \begin{cases} R_{i,\tau} - R_{f,\tau} & \text{if } R_{i,\tau} < R_{f,\tau} \\ 0 & \text{if } R_{i,\tau} > R_{f,\tau} \end{cases}$$

Using these semideviations, we calculate a Sortino ratio for each hedge fund index i for each month t:

$$\text{Sortino ratio}_{i,t} = \frac{R_{i,t} - R_{f,t}}{\text{Semideviation}_t} \qquad (4.3)$$

where $R_{i,t}$ denotes the average return of the hedge fund index i during the last 36 months, and $R_{f,t}$ denotes the risk-free rate at the end of month t. A greater Sortino ratio implies that the hedge fund index has generated a higher excess return per unit of downside risk. Since we calculate monthly Sortino ratios for each index, the following tables report the time series arithmetic averages of these Sortino ratios. Again, this methodology has the advantage of allowing for time variation in the downside risk-adjusted performances of hedge fund indices.

We begin our discussion with the Sortino ratios for the noninvestable DJCS hedge fund indices in Table 4.5. The full sample results indicate that, similar to the Sharpe ratios in Table 4.1, the equity market neutral index has the highest Sortino ratio which is equal to 1.196. In other words, this index has generated an excess return of about 1.2% per unit of semideviation. This finding deserves special attention because the equity market neutral index is the most negatively skewed and leptokurtic index in Table 3.1. Downside risk is a function of the higher order moments of a return distribution (see Cornish and Fisher (1937)); however, the extreme returns experienced by the equity market neutral index does not drag its average Sortino

Table 4.5 Sortino Ratios for DJCS Noninvestable Hedge Fund Indices

	Full Sample	Recent Sample
Event driven	0.45592	0.18636
Distressed restructuring	0.61399	0.19638
Merger/risk arbitrage	0.27199	0.32580
Multistrategy event driven	0.37443	0.18606
Long/short equity hedge	0.25603	0.14426
Equity market neutral	1.19577	0.22477
Dedicated short bias	− 0.08598	− 0.05885
Convertible arbitrage	0.22577	0.09876
Fixed-income arbitrage	0.21939	0.08252
Global macro	0.61670	0.41221
Emerging markets	0.18704	0.14711
Managed futures	0.10853	0.17392
Multistrategy	0.46079	0.17899
DJCS Hedge Fund Index	0.36524	0.18567
S&P 500 Index	0.08479	− 0.01094

ratio down. This finding also has to do with the fact that we calculate monthly Sortino ratios in a rolling window fashion. Although the negative extreme returns of the equity market neutral index during the recent credit crunch decreased the monthly Sortino ratios during the crisis period, the average Sortino ratio is still high due to the low volatility of the index outside this period.

After the equity market neutral index, the global macro index and the hedge fund indices in the event-driven category stand out with their high Sortino ratios. The global macro index has a Sortino ratio of 0.617, and four indices in the event-driven category have Sortino ratios between 0.272 and 0.614. With the exception of the merger/risk arbitrage index, all of these strategies outperform the DJCS Hedge Fund Index, which has a Sortino ratio of 0.365. The long/short equity hedge and dedicated short bias indices have low Sortino ratios, with the latter being the worst downside risk-adjusted performer with a Sortino ratio of −0.086. The managed futures and emerging markets indices follow the dedicated short bias index with Sortino ratios of 0.109 and 0.187. The fixed-income arbitrage and convertible arbitrage indices in the relative value category are also in the bottom half of the rankings with Sortino ratios of 0.219 and 0.226, respectively. The S&P 500 Index has a semideviation-adjusted performance of 0.085, which is about a quarter of that of the DJCS Hedge Fund Index and lower than those of all hedge fund indices except dedicated short bias.

In the recent sample, three indices, namely, the merger/risk arbitrage, dedicated short bias, and managed futures indices, have higher Sortino ratios compared to those in the full sample; however, most of the indices experience substantial drops in their downside risk-adjusted performances. Although the equity market neutral index still ranks in the top three, its Sortino ratio decreases substantially to 0.225. The global macro index leads the bunch with a Sortino ratio of 0.412, and the merger/risk arbitrage index joins the top three with a Sortino ratio of 0.326. The other indices in the event-driven category are also among the top half with their Sortino ratios clustered in a narrow band between 0.186 and 0.196. The dedicated short bias strategy is again the worst performer with a Sortino ratio of −0.056, and the convertible arbitrage and fixed-income arbitrage indices also perform weakly. These two indices in the relative value category have low mean returns and average volatilities in Table 3.2, and their negatively skewed and highly leptokurtic return distributions do not help for their downside risk-adjusted performances. The managed futures index experiences an improvement in its Sortino ratio during the recent sample, but it belongs to the bottom half of the rankings along with the emerging markets index. DJCS Hedge Fund Index would rank seventh among the strategy indices with its Sortino ratio of 0.186. The S&P 500 Index has a negative Sharpe ratio in Table 4.1, and it has a negative Sortino ratio of -0.011 here, which is only greater than that of the dedicated short bias strategy.

Table 4.6 presents Sortino ratios for investable DJCS indices. All investable indices have lower Sortino ratios compared to their noninvestable counterparts in Table 4.5. The exception is the managed futures index which also has the highest Sortino ratio of 0.195. Next is the event-driven index with its Sortino ratio of 0.136. Directional indices such as emerging markets and global macro also have comparatively strong downside risk-adjusted performances with Sortino ratios of 0.059 and 0.051. The equity hedge and the relative value categories yield poorly performing indices. The long/short equity hedge and dedicated short bias indices have negative Sortino ratios. In other words, the investable equity hedge funds have performed worse than their noninvestable counterparts in terms of downside risk-adjusted returns. A similar picture can be observed for the convertible arbitrage and

Table 4.6 Sortino Ratios for DJCS Investable Hedge Fund Indices	
	Recent Sample
Event driven	0.13602
Long/short equity hedge	0.01494
Equity market neutral	-0.04663
Dedicated short bias	-0.07547
Convertible arbitrage	0.03483
Fixed-income arbitrage	-0.08666
Global macro	0.05089
Emerging markets	0.05871
Managed futures	0.19513
Multistrategy	0.05458
DJCS AllHedge Index	0.05681
S&P 500 Index	-0.01512

fixed-income arbitrage indices, with the latter being at the bottom of the rankings with a Sortino ratio of -0.087. The investable DJCS All Hedge Fund Index would have ranked fourth among the strategy indices with its Sortino ratio of 0.057, whereas the S&P 500 Index can only beat the fixed-income arbitrage, dedicated short bias, and equity market neutral indices. In other words, despite their weak performances compared to noninvestable indices, some investable indices are able to outperform a traditional equity market benchmark in the recent period.

It is time to step back and reevaluate our discussion of the Sortino ratios for noninvestable and investable DJCS hedge fund indices. When we discussed the Sharpe ratio results earlier, we observed that telling a story solely based on mean returns is misleading. A hedge fund index with a high average return could turn out to be a mediocre volatility adjusted performer, and a hedge fund index with a low average return could turn out to be a strong volatility adjusted performer. This section is hinged on the idea that volatility may not be an adequate risk measure and adjusting returns with measures of downside risk has the potential to present a different picture. However, we observe that there are no substantial differences between the Sharpe ratio rankings in Tables 4.1 and 4.2 and the Sortino ratio rankings in Tables 4.5 and 4.6. One important difference is that the noninvestable equity market neutral index which ranks eighth based on its Sharpe ratio in the full sample now ranks first based on its Sortino ratio, but all other hedge fund indices move at most one or two spots up or down. In other words, controlling for semideviation around the risk-free rate rather than standard deviation around the mean return does not cause a monumental shift in the risk-adjusted performance rankings of hedge fund indices, despite the fact that many indices exhibit significant negative skewness and leptokurtosis. Our finding parallels that of Eling and Schuhmacher (2007), who find that, despite significant deviations of hedge fund returns from a normal distribution, the comparison of the Sharpe ratio to the other performance measures results in virtually identical rank ordering across hedge funds between 1985 and 2004. In our analysis, we focus on indices rather than individual hedge funds, and we extend the sample period; however, our results are consistent with those of Eling and Schuhmacher (2007). This does not mean that hedge fund investors can ignore downside risk and just concentrate on volatility. By doing so, investors would be underestimating the frequency of hedge fund failures and the exposure of their capital to extreme losses. The thing that does not matter much is just the comparative performances of hedge fund indices among each other.

Table 4.7 presents Sortino ratios for noninvestable HFRI indices. Based on the Sharpe ratios in Table 4.3, the fixed-income asset-backed arbitrage index has the best volatility adjusted performance. Here, we see that this index slips down to the sixth position with its Sortino ratio of 0.489 due to the large negative skewness and leptokurtosis of the index. Another index hurt by its extreme skewness and kurtosis

Table 4.7 Sortino Ratios for HFR Noninvestable Hedge Fund Indices		
	Full Sample	Recent Sample
Event driven	0.73102	0.10974
Distressed restructuring	0.84690	0.09521
Merger/risk arbitrage	0.39618	0.27292
Long/short equity hedge	0.41899	0.05830
Equity market neutral	0.53334	0.06889
Quantitative directional	0.26651	0.04964
Dedicated short bias	− 0.03290	0.04299
Energy/basic materials	0.31010	0.07991
Technology/health care	0.26804	0.17880
Relative value	0.77345	0.19642
Convertible arbitrage	0.39395	0.10333
Fixed-income corporate arbitrage	0.33107	0.04128
Fixed-income asset-backed arbitrage	0.48853	0.40796
Yield alternatives	0.24691	0.04405
Multistrategy relative value	0.68708	0.10148
Global macro	0.45454	0.40252
Systematic diversified	0.41336	0.37106
Emerging markets	0.29087	0.10884
Fund of funds composite	0.33031	0.02530
Fund of funds conservative	0.34287	0.02181
Fund of funds diversified	0.29643	0.02688
Fund of funds market defensive	0.31027	0.31654
Fund of funds strategic	0.26426	0.01893
HFRI Fund Weighted Composite Index	0.48159	0.12132
S&P 500 Index	0.10204	− 0.02604

statistics is also in the relative value category. The convertible arbitrage index slips from the sixth position based on Sharpe ratio rankings to the eleventh position with its Sortino ratio of 0.394. However, a large leptokurtosis does not impact the downside risk-adjusted performance of the relative value index adversely, and the index is able to retain its place in the top three, presumably due to its distribution's low asymmetry. Other indices in the relative value category such as the fixed-income corporate arbitrage and yield alternatives indices have both low Sharpe ratios and low Sortino ratios. The event-driven category hosts some indices that do better in Sortino ratio rankings compared to the Sharpe ratio rankings. The distressed restructuring index has the highest Sortino ratio of 0.847, and the event-driven index is in the top three with its Sortino ratio of 0.731. On the other hand, the merger/risk arbitrage index, which ranks fourth based on its Sharpe ratio, drops down to the tenth position, and we should note that this is one of the few indices whose kurtosis statistic is greater than 10. The indices in the equity hedge category are placed in the bottom half of the rankings except the equity market neutral index which has a Sortino ratio of 0.533. The global macro and systematic diversified indices populate the middle of the rankings, whereas the emerging markets index ranks even lower.

In the recent sample, the dedicated short bias and the market defensive fund of funds indices have higher Sortino ratios compared to the full sample. The fixed income asset-backed index has the best downside risk-adjusted performance with a Sortino ratio of 0.408 just as in the Sharpe ratio rankings in Table 4.3. The global macro and systematic diversified indices are next with Sortino ratios of 0.403 and 0.371, respectively. The indices in the event-driven category rank in the middle with the exception of the merger/arbitrage index which ranks fourth with its Sortino ratio of 0.273. The indices in the equity hedge category populate the bottom third of the rankings with Sortino ratios between 0.043 and 0.080 except the technology/health care index which ranks higher with its Sortino ratio of 0.179. The fixed-income corporate arbitrage and yield alternatives indices in the relative value category are in the bottom three with Sortino ratios of 0.041 and 0.044. The fund of funds indices have weak downside risk-adjusted performances and lower Sortino ratios compared to all strategy indices. The exception is the market defensive fund of funds index which would outperform all but three of the strategy indices with its Sortino ratio of 0.317. The HFRI Fund Weighted Composite Index would rank the seventh among the strategy indices, and the S&P 500 Index has a lower downside risk-adjusted performance with respect to all strategy indices with its Sortino ratio of −0.026.

Table 4.8 presents Sortino ratios for the HFRX investable hedge fund indices. Again, in the recent sample, we observe that most investable indices have lower Sortino ratios compared to their noninvestable counterparts. However, there are also several exceptions to this pattern. For example, the fixed-income corporate arbitrage, fixed-income asset-backed arbitrage, yield alternatives, and multistrategy relative value strategies under the relative value category have investable indices that generate higher Sortino ratios than the corresponding noninvestable indices. The same is true for the merger/risk arbitrage, technology/health care, and emerging markets indices. Note that the same exceptions were observed for Sharpe ratios in Table 4.4.

A strategy index that stands out in the Sortino ratio rankings is the commodity index, which has the eighth position based on the Sharpe ratio rankings. In Table 4.8, this index is the best downside risk-adjusted performer with a Sortino ratio of 0.498. The indices under the global macro category are collectively close to being asymmetric and exhibit low leptokurtosis. As a result, the active trading and multistrategy global macro indices under this category also find a place in the top five with their Sortino ratios 0.408 and 0.341. There is substantial heterogeneity in the event-driven category. On the one hand, the credit arbitrage and merger/risk arbitrage indices are in the top quintile among all other strategy indices with Sortino ratios of 0.408 and 0.285. On the other hand, distressed restructuring and event-driven indices rank toward the bottom with their negative average Sortino ratios. The indices under the equity hedge category generally perform poorly after downside risk adjustment and all of the indices here except technology/health care rank in the bottom half. The worst performers in this category are long/short equity hedge, equity market neutral, and fundamental value indices, which all exhibit negative Sortino ratios. A similar pattern is also observed for the relative value category, and all of the indices here have mediocre to poor downside risk-adjusted performances with the exception of the fixed-income asset-backed arbitrage index, which has the second highest Sortino ratio of 0.489. The worst performers in this category, namely, the

Table 4.8 Sortino Ratios for HFR Investable Hedge Fund Indices		
	Recent Sample	**Full Sample**
Event driven	− 0.00466	0.18345
Distressed restructuring	− 0.15377	0.21049
Merger/risk arbitrage	0.28460	0.21508
Credit arbitrage	0.40826	−
Activist	0.08991	−
Special situations	0.00734	−
Multistrategy event driven	0.19259	−
Long/short equity hedge	− 0.05805	0.26839
Equity market neutral	− 0.03551	−0.03302
Quantitative directional	0.03640	−
Dedicated short bias	0.00922	−
Fundamental growth	0.07799	−
Fundamental value	− 0.01994	−
Energy/basic materials	0.06325	−
Technology/health care	0.18666	−
Multistrategy equity hedge	0.09924	−
Relative value	− 0.00099	0.32854
Convertible arbitrage	− 0.05648	0.27889
Fixed-income corporate arbitrage	0.05843	−
Fixed-income sovereign arbitrage	0.08394	−
Fixed-income asset-backed arbitrage	0.48873	−
Yield alternatives	0.10450	−
Energy infrastructure	0.16667	−
Real estate	0.00816	−
Volatility	0.00465	0.08656
Multistrategy relative value	0.27973	−
Global macro	0.01345	0.19963
Discretionary thematic	0.15113	−
Systematic diversified	0.28083	−
Active trading	0.40753	−
Currency	0.00461	−
Commodity	0.49814	−
Agriculture	0.21991	−
Energy	0.00154	−
Metals	0.24854	−
Multistrategy global macro	0.34098	−

(*Continued*)

Table 4.8 (Continued)		
	Recent Sample	Full Sample
Emerging markets	0.19509	–
HFRX Global Hedge Fund Index	– 0.02743	0.26833
HFRX Equal Weighted Strategies Index	– 0.02193	0.34277
HFRX Absolute Return Index	– 0.12980	0.22156
HFRX Market Directional Index	0.01731	0.18885
S&P 500 Index	– 0.02604	0.00743

relative value and convertible arbitrage indices, are also the indices that have the highest kurtosis statistics in Table 3.6. All the composite indices except the HFRX Market Directional Index have negative Sortino ratios. The S&P 500 Index also has a negative Sortino ratio of -0.026, but the performance difference between the S&P 500 and the hedge fund indices has closed down.

When we focus on the investable indices for which data is available for a longer sample period, we do not spot any new patterns except that the event-driven category experiences a small decline in its performance, whereas the relative value and convertible arbitrage indices surpass them with Sortino ratios of 0.329 and 0.279. The equity market neutral and volatility indices are at the bottom of the rankings with Sortino ratios of -0.033 and 0.087, respectively.

To recap, we do not observe considerable differences between the Sharpe ratio and the Sortino ratio rankings for the HFR indices. Despite some exceptions such as the commodity index which climbs seven spots in the Sortino ratio rankings, a vast majority of the hedge fund indices move up or down at most three positions. The highly negatively skewed or leptokurtic index distributions do not get penalized heavily, and the less skewed and leptokurtic distributions are not rewarded above and beyond what their volatility statistics imply.

4.3 RETURN TO VAR RATIO

The similarities between the Sharpe ratio and the Sortino ratio rankings may be driven by the similarities in the way that the standard deviation and semideviation statistics are constructed. The Sharpe ratio reflects the dispersion of both high and low returns around the mean, whereas the Sortino ratio reflects the dispersion of only the low returns around the risk-free rate. In other words, the latter ratio is focused on the left tail of the index return distribution and utilizes a different benchmark. However, the bottom line is that both risk measures are based on squared deviations around a target return. Thus, in this section, we use a more sophisticated measure of downside risk and investigate whether this measure creates any changes in our inferences.

An alternative to the semideviation as a measure of downside risk is the value at risk (VaR). VaR attempts to answer the question of how much an investor can expect to lose on a portfolio in a given time period at a given level of probability. For example, if a portfolio of equities has a 1-month 5% VaR of -20%, this means that there is a 5% probability that the portfolio value will decline by more than 20% over a 1-month period. For a normal distribution, VaR does not add any more information to what the standard deviation already reflects.

In our empirical treatment, we use a parametric measure of VaR which is constructed in the following way. To account for skewness and excess kurtosis in the data, Hansen (1994) introduces a generalization of the Student t-distribution where asymmetries may occur while maintaining the assumption of a zero mean and unit variance. This skewed t (ST) density is given by

$$
f(z_t; \mu, \sigma, v, \lambda) =
\begin{cases}
bc\left(1 + \frac{1}{v-2}\left(\frac{bz_t+a}{1-\lambda}\right)^2\right)^{-\frac{v+1}{2}} & \text{if } z_t < -a/b \\[3mm]
bc\left(1 + \frac{1}{v-2}\left(\frac{bz_t+a}{1+\lambda}\right)^2\right)^{-\frac{v+1}{2}} & \text{if } z_t \geq -a/b
\end{cases}
\tag{4.4}
$$

where $z_t = \frac{R_t - \mu}{\sigma}$ is the standardized expected market return, and the constants a, b, and c are given by

$$
a = 4\lambda c\left(\frac{v-2}{v-1}\right), \quad b^2 = 1 + 3\lambda^2 - a^2, \quad c = \frac{\Gamma\left(\frac{v+1}{2}\right)}{\sqrt{\pi(v-2)}\Gamma\left(\frac{v}{2}\right)}
\tag{4.5}
$$

Hansen (1994) shows that this density is defined for $2 < v < \infty$ and $-1 < \lambda < 1$. This density has a single mode at $-a/b$, which is of opposite sign with the parameter λ. Thus, if $\lambda > 0$, the mode of the density is to the left of zero and the variable is skewed to the right, and vice versa when $\lambda < 0$. Furthermore, if $\lambda = 0$, Hansen's distribution reduces to the traditional standardized t-distribution. If $\lambda = 0$ and $v = \infty$, it reduces to a normal density.

The parameters of the ST density are estimated by maximizing the log-likelihood function of R_t with respect to the parameters μ, σ, v and λ:

$$\log L = n\ln b + n\ln \Gamma\left(\frac{v+1}{2}\right) - \frac{n}{2}\ln \pi - n\ln \Gamma(v-2) - n\ln \Gamma\left(\frac{v}{2}\right) - n\ln \sigma$$
$$- \left(\frac{v+1}{2}\right) \sum_{t=1}^{n} \ln\left(1 + \frac{d_t^2}{(v-2)}\right)$$

where $d_t = (bz_t + a)/(1 - \lambda s)$ and s is a sign dummy taking the value of 1 if $bz_t + a < 0$ and $s = -1$ otherwise.

The parametric approach to calculating VaR is based on the lower tail of the ST distribution. Specifically, we estimate the parameters of the ST density (μ, σ, v, λ) using the past 36 months of return data and then find the corresponding percentile of the estimated distribution. Assuming that $R_t = f_{v,\lambda}(z)$ follows a ST density, parametric VaR is the solution to

$$\int_{-\infty}^{\Gamma_{ST}(\Phi)} f_{v,\lambda}(z)\mathrm{d}z = \Phi \qquad (4.6)$$

where $\Gamma_{ST}(\Phi)$ is the VaR threshold based on the ST density with a loss probability of Φ. Equation (4.6) indicates that VaR can be calculated by integrating the area under the probability density function of the ST distribution given by Bali et al. (2009). The degree of significance that we choose for the VaR measure is 1%.[1]

Once we calculate a parametric VaR value for each hedge fund index i for each month t, we calculate the return to VaR ratios in a rolling window fashion using the following formula:

$$\text{Return to VaR}_{i,t} = \frac{R_{i,t} - R_{f,t}}{|\text{VaR}_t|} \qquad (4.7)$$

---

[1] An alternative approach to estimating VaR is based on extreme value distributions and parametric density forecasts. See McNeil and Frey (2000), Berkowitz (2001), Berkowitz and O'Brian (2002), Bali (2003, 2007), Bali and Weinbaum (2007), and Bali and Theodossiou (2007, 2008).

Table 4.9 Return to VaR Ratios for DJCS Noninvestable Hedge Fund Indices		
	Full Sample	Recent Sample
Event driven	0.28620	0.10400
Distressed restructuring	0.51068	0.10322
Merger/risk arbitrage	0.14241	0.17665
Multistrategy event driven	0.22218	0.10016
Long/short equity hedge	0.12753	0.06980
Equity market neutral	0.83757	0.26652
Dedicated short bias	− 0.04454	− 0.02682
Convertible arbitrage	0.24269	0.05223
Fixed-income arbitrage	0.19657	0.05592
Global macro	0.37558	0.23688
Emerging markets	0.09745	0.07002
Managed futures	0.05049	0.08330
Multistrategy	0.25897	0.09375
DJCS Hedge Fund Index	0.18615	0.09692
S&P 500 Index	0.04558	− 0.00258

where $R_{i,t}$ denotes the average return of the hedge fund index i during the last 36 months, and $R_{f,t}$ denotes the risk-free rate at the end of month t. Absolute values are necessary in the denominator because VaR is a negative number and we want to define our risk-adjusted performance measures such that a higher value corresponds to a better performance.

Our goal in this section is to investigate whether using VaR as an alternative downside risk measure will change the comparative risk-adjusted performances of the hedge fund indices. We will just summarize the similar patterns and pinpoint the differences if there are any. Table 4.9 presents return to VaR ratios for the noninvestable DJCS indices. The magnitudes of these ratios and the magnitudes of the Sortino ratios in Table 4.5 are, of course, different. However, the three indices with the best downside risk-adjusted performances are still the equity market neutral, distressed restructuring, and global macro indices with return to VaR ratios between 0.376 and 0.838. The three worst performers are again the dedicated short bias, managed futures, and emerging markets indices with return to VaR ratios between − 0.045 and 0.098. DJCS Hedge Fund Index would rank ninth among the strategy indices with a return to VaR ratio of 0.186, and the S&P

Table 4.10 Return to VaR Ratios for DJCS Investable Hedge Fund Indices	Recent Sample
Event driven	0.06864
Long/short equity hedge	0.01154
Equity market neutral	− 0.00216
Dedicated short bias	− 0.03028
Convertible arbitrage	0.02580
Fixed-income arbitrage	− 0.03307
Global macro	0.02363
Emerging markets	0.03512
Managed futures	0.09586
Multistrategy	0.07049
DJCS All Hedge Index	0.03399
S&P 500 Index	− 0.00488

500 Index again underperforms all strategy indices except dedicated short bias. In the recent sample, the three indices with improved downside risk-adjusted performances are again the merger/risk arbitrage, dedicated short bias, and managed futures indices. The indices that stand out with their high return to VaR ratios are the equity market neutral index and the indices under the event-driven category. The worst performers are again the long/short equity hedge and dedicated short bias strategies in the equity hedge category and the convertible arbitrage and fixed-income arbitrage indices in the relative value category. For the investable DJCS indices presented in Table 4.10, the only strategy that exhibits a better investable index performance compared to Table 4.9 is the managed futures strategy, which also has the highest return to VaR ratio of 0.096. Other indices with high return to VaR ratios are multistrategy and event-driven indices. The equity hedge and relative value categories again populate the bottom of the rankings. To summarize, our inferences from Tables 4.9 and 4.10 are very similar to our inferences from the Sortino ratio results. The rankings based on VaR parallel those that are based on semideviation as a risk measure. It seems that the point raised by Eling and Schuhmacher (2007) is valid for hedge fund indices and in a more recent sample period.

Nevertheless, we go on and report the return to VaR ratios for noninvestable HFR indices in Table 4.11. The distressed restructuring

Table 4.11 Return to VaR Ratios for HFR Noninvestable Hedge Fund Indices		
	Full Sample	Recent Sample
Event driven	0.44152	0.05314
Distressed restructuring	1.23058	0.04791
Merger/risk arbitrage	0.30032	0.14082
Long/short equity hedge	0.22190	0.02905
Equity market neutral	1.03185	0.04009
Quantitative directional	0.13192	0.02508
Dedicated short bias	− 0.01490	0.02150
Energy/basic materials	0.16121	0.03884
Technology/health care	0.12946	0.08410
Relative value	0.53625	0.10377
Convertible arbitrage	0.36143	0.04829
Fixed-income corporate arbitrage	0.26197	0.02451
Fixed-income asset-backed arbitrage	0.74148	0.23092
Yield alternatives	0.12933	0.02735
Multistrategy relative value	0.75539	0.04721
Global macro	0.23381	0.18858
Systematic diversified	0.21535	0.16810
Emerging markets	0.16172	0.05733
Fund of funds composite	0.22668	0.01759
Fund of funds conservative	0.22740	0.01411
Fund of funds diversified	0.17863	0.01786
Fund of funds market defensive	0.16423	0.14939
Fund of funds strategic	0.15480	0.01404
HFRI Fund Weighted Composite Index	0.27224	0.05988
S&P 500 Index	0.05412	− 0.01051

index which has the highest Sortino ratio in Table 4.7 leads other strategy indices with its return to VaR ratio of 1.231. The equity market neutral index exhibits some improvement with respect to Table 4.7 and has the second-highest return to VaR ratio of 1.032. However, we should note that this high average return to VaR ratio is driven by several observations in excess of 20 during the second half of 1998. Without these outliers, the average Sortino ratio of the equity market neutral index would be 0.464. Other indices in the equity hedge category have low return to VaR ratios. The indices under the event-driven category other than distressed restructuring are also in the top half of the return to VaR ratio rankings. The relative value, multistrategy relative value, and fixed-income asset-backed arbitrage indices are among the top five. In contrast, the yield alternatives index in the same category has the second lowest return to VaR ratio of 0.129. Looking at the recent sample, we observe sharp declines in the rankings of the distressed restructuring, equity market neutral, fixed-income corporate arbitrage, and multistrategy relative value indices. Their places are taken by the technology/health care, global macro, systematic diversified, and emerging markets indices that record substantial improvements. The HFRI Fund Weighted Composite Index has a return to VaR ratio in the recent sample, which is one quarter of what it is in the full sample. The S&P 500 Index is the only index with a negative average return to VaR ratio in the recent sample. All of these patterns were noted for the Sortino ratios in Table 4.7.

Finally, we discuss the results for the investable HFRX indices in Table 4.12. The six indices with the highest return to VaR ratios are exactly the same as the six indices with the highest Sortino ratios in Table 4.8. The strong performers are the commodity and active trading indices under the global macro category, the credit arbitrage and merger/risk arbitrage indices under the event-driven category, and the fixed income asset-backed arbitrage index. The weakest performers are the long/short equity hedge, equity market neutral indices, distressed restructuring, and convertible arbitrage indices. Four of the HFRX composite indices, except market directional and the S&P 500 Index again have negative average return to VaR ratios. The investable indices that perform better than their noninvestable counterparts are exactly the same with those in Table 4.8. The conclusion is that VaR does not provide any additional insight beyond semideviation as far as the risk-adjusted performance rankings of hedge fund indices are concerned.

The historical downside risk-adjusted performances of the HFRI Fund Weighted Composite Index, Fund of Funds Composite Index, and S&P 500 Index are presented in Figures 4.5 and 4.6. We observe that the S&P 500 Index is dominated by the hedge fund indices; however, the most pronounced outperformance occurs in the first half of the 1990s, and there have been no significant performance differences between the three indices since the 2008 financial crisis. Another observation is that the large drops in mean returns during the recent crisis cannot be observed for the downside risk-adjusted performances.

Table 4.12 Return to VaR Ratios for HFR Investable Hedge Fund Indices		
	Recent Sample	Full Sample
Event driven	0.00057	0.09296
Distressed restructuring	− 0.04535	0.11875
Merger/risk arbitrage	0.16032	0.11600
Credit arbitrage	0.21931	−
Activist	0.04193	−
Special situations	0.00706	−
Multistrategy Event Driven	0.08929	−
Long/short equity hedge	− 0.01728	0.89657
Equity market neutral	− 0.01444	−0.01186
Quantitative directional	0.02057	−
Dedicated short bias	0.00504	−
Fundamental growth	0.04383	−
Fundamental value	− 0.00128	−
Energy/basic materials	0.03373	−
Technology/health care	0.08082	−
Multistrategy equity hedge	0.05023	−
Relative value	0.00164	0.22616
Convertible arbitrage	− 0.01954	0.17644
Fixed-income corporate arbitrage	0.03250	−
Fixed-income sovereign arbitrage	0.03673	−
Fixed-income asset-backed arbitrage	0.27570	−
Yield alternatives	0.04941	−
Energy infrastructure	0.07754	−
Real estate	0.00310	−
Volatility	0.03185	0.05977
Multistrategy relative value	0.12788	−
Global macro	0.00456	0.09647
Discretionary thematic	0.06386	−
Systematic diversified	0.13522	−
Active trading	0.19716	−
Currency	0.00166	−
Commodity	0.31342	−
Agriculture	0.12123	−
Energy	0.00298	−
Metals	0.10957	−
Multistrategy global macro	0.15672	−

(Continued)

Table 4.12 (Continued)		
	Recent Sample	Full Sample
Emerging markets	0.08229	–
HFRX Global Hedge Fund Index	– 0.00551	0.15779
HFRX Equal Weighted Strategies Index	– 0.00312	0.26464
HFRX Absolute Return Index	– 0.04451	0.14200
HFRX Market Directional Index	0.01149	0.08979
S&P 500 Index	– 0.01051	0.00632

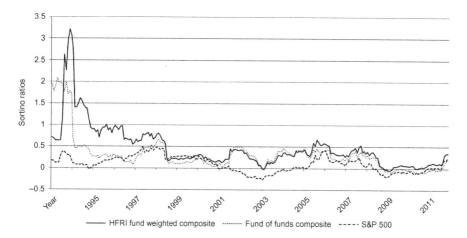

Figure 4.5 Sortino ratios for HFRI fund weighted composite, fund of funds composite, and S&P 500 indices

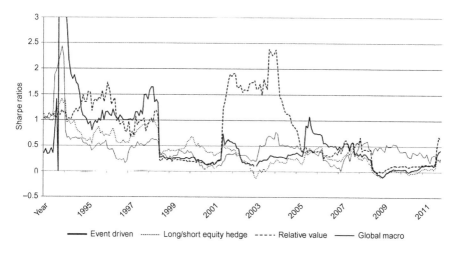

Figure 4.6 Return to VaR ratios for HFRI fund weighted composite, fund of funds composite, and S&P 500 indices

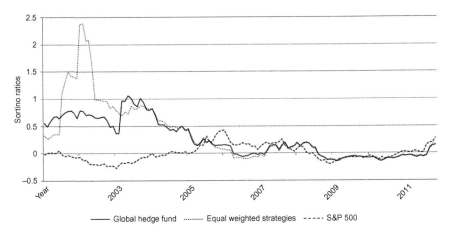

Figure 4.7 Sortino ratios for HFRI event driven, long/short equity hedge, relative value, and global macro indices

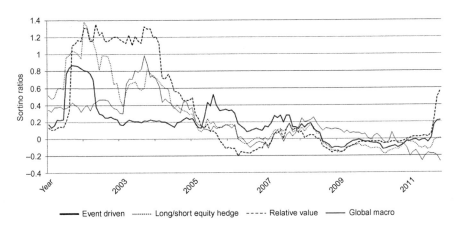

Figure 4.8 Return to VaR ratios for HFRI event driven, long/short equity, relative value, and global macro indices

Figures 4.7 and 4.8 present the same performance metrics for various noninvestable strategy indices. For the event-driven index, there are some outliers at the end of 1993 with Sortino ratios that exceed 10. If we were to delete these observations, the average Sortino ratio of the event-driven index would decrease from 0.731 to 0.539, but it would still be a decent performer. The same would hold for the return to VaR ratios as well. The long/short equity hedge index does exceptionally well between 2002 and 2005. Again, there have been no drastic deteriorations in downside risk-adjusted performance during the 2008 crisis, but we can observe that the global macro index experienced the crisis relatively more unscathed.

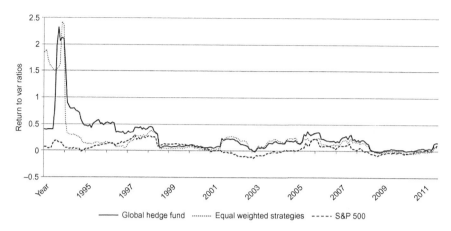

Figure 4.9 Sortino ratios for HFRX global hedge fund, equal weighted strategies, and S&P 500 indices

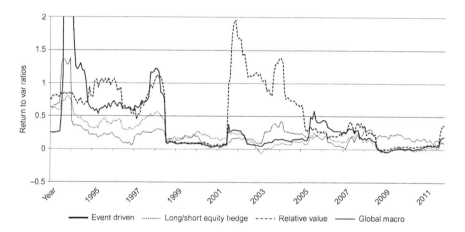

Figure 4.10 Return to VaR ratios for HFRX global hedge fund, equal weighted strategies, and S&P 500 indices

Figures 4.9 and 4.10 present the historical downside risk-adjusted performances of the HFRX Global Hedge Fund, HFRX Equal Weighted Strategies, and S&P 500 indices. We observe that the Equal Weighted Strategies Index is dominant during the first years of the 2000s, and the two composite hedge fund indices experienced a decline in their Sortino and return to VaR ratios around 2005. Since then, there have been no visible performance differences between the three indices. Figures 4.11 and 4.12 present the same performance metrics for various investable strategy indices. The Sortino ratios reach their peaks for all four strategy indices during the first half of the 2000s, and these peaks are most pronounced for the long/short equity hedge

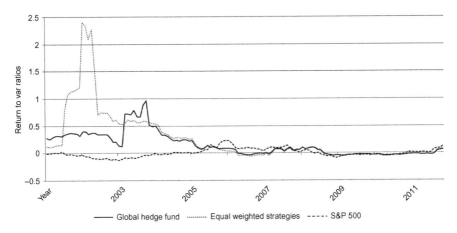

Figure 4.11 Sortino ratios for HFRX event driven, long/short equity hedge, relative value, and global macro indices

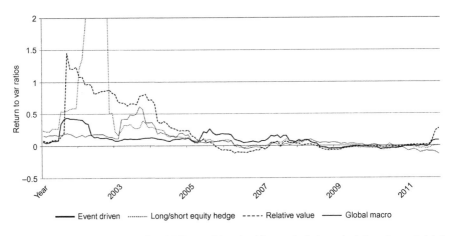

Figure 4.12 Return to VaR ratios for HFRX event driven, long/short equity hedge and relative value, and global macro indices

and relative value indices. There is a convergence in Sortino ratios around 2005, after which first the event-driven and then the global macro indices dominate the others for brief periods of time. At the end of the sample period, we see spikes in downside risk-adjusted performance, especially for the relative value index. Similar patterns exist for the return to VaR ratios, and the most recognizable difference is that the long/short equity index exhibits some outliers during 2002. If we were to remove these outliers, the average Sortino ratio of the long/short equity hedge index would decline from 0.897 to 0.178, but it would still rank second among the handful of investable indices for which we can obtain a longer data series.

4.4 CALMAR RATIO

Another common risk measure used in the asset management industry is the drawdown. Drawdown reflects the percentage decline in the value of an asset or an index from its historical peak or highest level. A behavioral interpretation of drawdown is the regret that an investor would feel for not selling an asset at its peak or redeeming his or her capital from a fund at its most valuable point. We calculate a measure called the maximum drawdown as the percentage difference between the highest and the lowest values of a hedge fund index during the last 36 months. Then, we construct a Calmar ratio for each hedge fund index i for each month t in the following way:

$$\text{Calmar ratio}_{i,t} = \frac{R_{i,t}}{\text{Maximum drawdown}_t} \qquad (4.8)$$

where $R_{i,t}$ denotes the annualized return that hedge fund index i generates during the last 36 months. Maximum drawdown is sensitive to the estimation methodology. If the frequency of the measurement interval is smaller or the time series for which maximum drawdown computed is longer, the maximum drawdown statistic will be mechanically larger. Our methodology ensures that the maximum drawdown statistics are comparable across indices. Again, since we calculate monthly Calmar ratios for each index, the tables will report the time-series arithmetic averages of these Calmar ratios. In our earlier discussions, we pointed out that rankings based on Sortino and return to VaR ratios produce similar results to each other as well as to the Sharpe ratio rankings. Our goal here is to explore whether the comparison of the Calmar ratio to the Sharpe ratio results in identical rank ordering across hedge fund indices.

Table 4.13 presents Calmar ratios for noninvestable DJCS hedge fund indices. In the full sample, the highest Calmar ratio is equal to 0.362, and it belongs to the global macro index, which ranks third based on Sharpe ratios in Table 4.1. The second- and third-highest Calmar ratios belong to the merger/risk arbitrage and multistrategy event-driven indices, which rank eighth and sixth based on Sharpe ratios, respectively. In other words, there are some index changes at the top of

Table 4.13 Calmar Ratios for DJCS Noninvestable Hedge Fund Indices		
	Full Sample	Recent Sample
Event driven	0.33255	0.20054
Distressed restructuring	0.32469	0.14199
Merger/risk arbitrage	0.33590	0.30523
Multistrategy event driven	0.33435	0.23591
Long/short equity hedge	0.29302	0.15849
Equity market neutral	0.26303	− 0.07608
Dedicated short bias	− 0.08052	− 0.06350
Convertible arbitrage	0.28595	0.11121
Fixed-income arbitrage	0.25120	0.05660
Global macro	0.36193	0.32520
Emerging markets	0.22039	0.15324
Managed futures	0.25558	0.27636
Multistrategy	0.31830	0.14122
DJCS Hedge Fund Index	0.32314	0.17476
S&P 500 Index	0.14381	− 0.02395

the rankings, and some funds exhibit upward mobility based on Calmar ratios. Aside from the merger/risk arbitrage index, other indices in the event-driven category also exhibit favorable performance. The event-driven and distressed restructuring indices have Calmar ratios of 0.335 and 0.325, respectively. The long/short equity and equity market neutral indices are positioned in the middle with Calmar ratios of 0.293 and 0.263. The three indices with the lowest Sharpe ratios in Table 4.1 are the dedicated short bias, managed futures, and emerging markets indices, and these indices are again at the bottom in the Calmar ratio rankings. So, it is not possible to talk about a radically different rank ordering among hedge fund indices. DJCS Hedge Fund Index would rank sixth among the strategy indices, and the S&P 500 Index can only outperform the dedicated short bias index with its Calmar ratio of 0.144. In the recent sample, the dedicated short bias and managed futures indices improve their Calmar ratios as was the case for the other risk-adjusted performance metrics. The global macro index is the top performer, the indices under the event-driven category perform favorably and the indices under the equity hedge and relative value categories populate the bottom half of the rankings. One particular index that visibly climbs up the rankings in the recent period is the managed futures

Table 4.14 Calmar Ratios for DJCS Investable Hedge Fund Indices	
	Recent Sample
Event driven	0.13405
Long/short equity hedge	− 0.00073
Equity market neutral	− 0.12069
Dedicated short bias	− 0.14343
Convertible arbitrage	− 0.01113
Fixed-income arbitrage	− 0.14794
Global macro	0.06842
Emerging markets	0.03410
Managed futures	0.29575
Multistrategy	− 0.00537
DJCS AllHedge Index	0.03546
S&P 500 Index	− 0.03216

index which gains seven spots and moves into the third rank with a Calmar ratio of 0.276. Table 4.14 presents Calmar ratios for investable DJCS hedge fund indices. All of the investable indices, except the managed futures index, have lower Calmar ratios compared to their noninvestable counterparts. The managed futures index has the highest Calmar ratio which is equal to 0.296. The event-driven, global macro, and emerging markets indices perform strongly, whereas the indices under the equity hedge and relative value categories perform weakly. The investable DJCS AllHedge Index has a Calmar ratio of 0.035, which is one fifth of that of the noninvestable DJCS Hedge Fund Index. However, DJCS AllHedge Index would still rank fourth among all investable strategy indices. The S&P 500 Index has a negative average Calmar ratio of − 0.032, which is greater than those of only three strategy indices.

The remarkable thing about all these results is that the patterns are very similar to what we observe in Tables 4.1 and 4.2 for Sharpe ratios. Aside from some particular exceptions detailed above, most hedge fund indices do not move more than one or two spots in the Calmar ratio rankings. We could have copied and pasted our discussion for Sharpe ratios here, and it would have been hard to spot the inconsistencies. In Chapter 3, we made the point that the range is the most primitive risk measure. The risk measure in the denominator of

Table 4.15 Calmar Ratios for HFR Noninvestable Hedge Fund Indices		
	Full Sample	Recent Sample
Event driven	0.34846	0.11253
Distressed restructuring	0.34397	0.08905
Merger/risk arbitrage	0.36707	0.28348
Long/short equity hedge	0.32937	0.06126
Equity market neutral	0.31552	0.06483
Quantitative directional	0.29484	0.05113
Dedicated short bias	− 0.00160	0.01805
Energy/basic materials	0.30895	0.06308
Technology/health care	0.31556	0.22532
Relative value	0.36177	0.20082
Convertible arbitrage	0.31905	0.11273
Fixed-income corporate arbitrage	0.28378	0.06261
Fixed-income asset-backed arbitrage	0.34102	0.33037
Yield alternatives	0.26613	0.04624
Multistrategy relative value	0.32394	0.09929
Global macro	0.39406	0.32905
Systematic diversified	0.38243	0.34666
Emerging markets	0.29132	0.11384
Fund of funds composite	0.28830	0.01828
Fund of funds conservative	0.29494	0.00057
Fund of funds diversified	0.27971	0.02098
Fund of funds market defensive	0.35190	0.30568
Fund of funds strategic	0.26367	0.01141
HFRI Fund Weighted Composite Index	0.34293	0.13238
S&P 500 Index	0.18689	− 0.05357

the Calmar ratio is a percentage range, and this simple measure produces virtually the same rankings as the Sharpe ratio which has the standard deviation in its denominator.

Table 4.15 presents the Calmar ratios for noninvestable HFRI indices. The highest Calmar ratios belong to the global macro and systematic diversified indices and are equal to 0.394 and 0.382, respectively. This is not the case for the full sample Sharpe ratio rankings in Table 4.3 where the two indices are positioned in the middle. The three indices under the event-driven category follow next with Calmar ratios between 0.344 and 0.367. The indices under the equity hedge category retain their places in the bottom half of the rankings. The best performer in this category is the long/short equity hedge index with a Calmar ratio of 0.329, and the worst performer in this category is the dedicated short bias index with a Calmar ratio of -0.002. The indices under the relative value category lose some spots compared to the Sharpe ratio rankings. The best performer in this category is the relative value index, which ranks fourth overall with a Calmar ratio of 0.362, and all other indices in this category exhibit poor to mediocre performances. The two indices which lose the most ranks based on Calmar ratios are the fixed-income asset backed and multistrategy relative value indices. One should also note that the yield alternative index, which has the second-worst performance, has a Calmar ratio of 0.266 — two thirds of that of the global macro index. In other words, the Calmar ratios are clustered in a tight range, and the rankings are decided by small differences. The Calmar ratio does not have the same differentiating power among indices as the Sharpe ratio and downside risk-adjusted performance metrics do. Keeping this in mind, the market defensive fund of funds index would have ranked the fifth among the strategy indices with its Calmar ratio of 0.352, whereas all other fund of funds indices would place in the bottom quartile. HFRI Fund Weighted Composite Index would have ranked seventh among the strategy indices with its Calmar ratio of 0.343, whereas S&P 500 Index would only outperform the dedicated short bias index.

In the recent sample, as is customary, there is a drop in Calmar ratios for all indices except the dedicated short bias index. The top performers are again the global macro and systematic diversified indices with Calmar ratios of 0.347 and 0.329, respectively. The fixed-income asset-backed arbitrage index joins them with its Calmar ratio of 0.330. The merger/risk arbitrage index ranks fourth, but the other indices in the event-driven category rank somewhere in the middle. Except the technology/healthcare index, the indices in the equity hedge category populate the bottom tercile with Calmar ratios between 0.018 and 0.065. The relative value category is heterogeneous. The yield alternatives index has the worst performance after the dedicated short bias index; however, the relative value and convertible arbitrage indices are in the top half of the rankings. Also, the emerging markets index improves its comparative performance during the recent period and moves up to the seventh rank. The fund of funds indices underperform all strategy indices with the exception of the market defensive fund of funds index which has a Calmar ratio of 0.306. The HFRI Fund Weighted Composite Index would have ranked seventh among the strategy indices, whereas the S&P 500 Index is the only index that has a negative average Calmar ratio.

Table 4.16 presents the Calmar ratios for investable HFRX indices. If we proceed category by category, the indices under the event-driven category rank in the bottom half except the merger/risk arbitrage and credit arbitrage indices which have Calmar ratios of 0.334 and 0.309, respectively. The worst Calmar ratio is -0.172 and belongs to the distressed restructuring index. All the indices under the equity hedge category are also in the bottom half of the rankings except the technology/ health care index. The highest Calmar ratio of 0.384 belongs to the fixed-income asset-backed arbitrage index, which is under the relative value category. The multistrategy relative value index also has a favorable Calmar ratio of 0.280, but the rest of the indices in this category exhibit poor to mediocre performances. A majority of the indices in the global macro category rank in the top tercile with the metals, global macro, and active trading indices placing in the top five with their Calmar ratios between 0.383 and 0.315. Three of the investable composite hedge fund indices have negative average Calmar ratios which are close to that of the S&P 500 Index. To summarize the results from Tables 4.15 and 4.16, the HFR indices also confirm the conjecture that the Calmar ratio does not provide a substantial amount of extra information for hedge fund index rankings.

Figures 4.13 and 4.14 exhibit the historical Calmar ratios for selected noninvestable HFRI indices. We observe that the HFRI Fund Weighted Composite Index and Fund of Funds Composite Index move in tandem with a correlation coefficient of 0.95. Although the S&P Index underperforms these two hedge fund indices, especially between 2002 and 2005 and during the 2008 financial crisis, the correlation between the S&P 500 Index and the two hedge fund indices is at least 0.59. We also observe that the four noninvestable strategy indices are highly correlated among each other. The pairwise correlations between all strategy indices except the global macro index are between 0.84 and 0.91. The pairwise correlations between the global macro index and the other strategy indices are also high and at least equal to 0.51. One thing that stands out is the dramatic fall in its Calmar ratio that the long/short equity hedge index experiences in 2003. Also, the

Table 4.16 Calmar Ratios for HFR Investable Hedge Fund Indices		
	Recent Sample	Full Sample
Event driven	− 0.00749	0.22015
Distressed restructuring	− 0.17151	0.17586
Merger/risk arbitrage	0.33362	–
Credit arbitrage	0.30876	–
Activist	0.08938	–
Special situations	− 0.00910	–
Multistrategy event driven	0.10552	–
Long/short equity hedge	− 0.08005	0.20740
Equity market neutral	− 0.03161	0.09338
Quantitative directional	0.01984	–
Dedicated short bias	− 0.00019	–
Fundamental growth	0.08428	–
Fundamental value	− 0.05953	–
Energy/basic materials	0.05008	–
Technology/health care	0.25362	–
Multistrategy equity hedge	0.11369	–
Relative value	− 0.01288	0.22383
Convertible arbitrage	− 0.15935	0.11205
Fixed-income corporate arbitrage	0.05670	–
Fixed-income sovereign arbitrage	0.08628	–
Fixed-income asset-backed arbitrage	0.38357	–
Yield alternatives	0.11753	–
Energy infrastructure	0.16666	–
Real estate	0.02743	–
Volatility	0.05569	0.11244
Multistrategy relative value	0.28043	–
Global macro	0.02791	0.23416
Discretionary thematic	0.20326	–
Systematic diversified	0.29553	–
Active trading	0.31503	–
Currency	0.04478	–
Commodity	0.20326	–
Agriculture	0.20390	–
Energy	− 0.02036	–
Metals	0.38313	–
Multistrategy global macro	0.32533	–

(*Continued*)

Table 4.16 (Continued)		
	Recent Sample	**Full Sample**
Emerging markets	0.23400	–
HFRX Global Hedge Fund Index	− 0.04076	0.22294
HFRX Equal Weighted Strategies Index	− 0.03879	0.21913
HFRX Absolute Return Index	− 0.12618	0.18225
HFRX Market Directional Index	0.01199	0.23307
S&P 500 Index	− 0.05357	0.02609

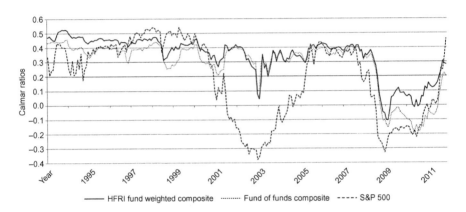

Figure 4.13 Calmar ratios for HFRI fund weighted composite, fund of funds composite, and S&P 500 indices

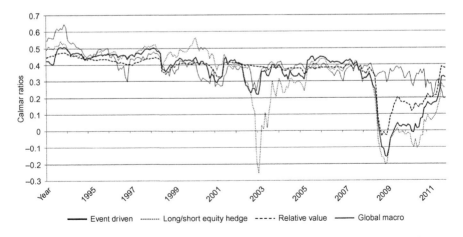

Figure 4.14 Calmar ratios for HFRI event driven, long/short equity hedge, relative value, and global macro indices

adverse impact of the 2008 crisis and the subsequent comebacks are readily visible. The index that had the least damage during this period seems to be the global macro index.

Figures 4.15 and 4.16 exhibit the historical Calmar ratios for selected investable HFRX indices. The two composite hedge fund indices are virtually indistinguishable from each other, and they have a correlation of 0.996. The pairwise correlation between these two indices and the S&P index is 0.31, which is comparatively low. However, this low correlation is driven by the fact that the S&P 500 Index exhibits negative Calmar ratios during the first half of the 2000s. The

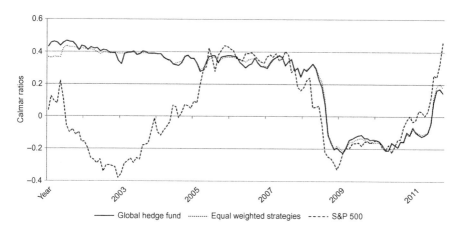

Figure 4.15 Calmar ratios for HFRX global hedge fund, equal weighted strategies, and S&P 500 indices

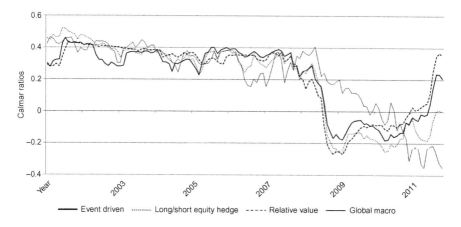

Figure 4.16 Calmar ratios for HFRX event driven, long/short equity hedge, relative value, and global macro indices

Calmar ratios for all three indices converge during 2005, decline during the 2008 crisis, and revert back later. During the sample period after 2005, the correlation between the S&P 500 Index and the composite hedge fund indices goes up to 0.90. This is alarming in terms of the diversification benefits of investing in hedge funds. We also observe a general downward trend in the Calmar ratios of the investable strategy indices. The pairwise correlations between all strategy indices except the global macro index are between 0.92 and 0.96. The pairwise correlations between the global macro index and the other strategy indices are between 0.60 and 0.82. Although the global macro index dodges the recent credit crunch with fewer scars, it experiences a decline just as the other strategy indices recuperate themselves.

Determinants of Hedge Fund Index Returns

In Chapter 1, we introduced some fund-specific factors such as a hedge fund's fee structure and size and liquidity characteristics such as the existence of lock-up periods as determinants of individual hedge fund returns in our literature review. In this chapter, we investigate the determinants of hedge fund index returns through two channels. First, motivated by the recent interest in higher-order moments in explaining asset returns, we test whether the moments of the hedge fund index return distributions can predict the cross-sectional differences in future hedge fund index returns. Second, we calculate the sensitivities or the exposures of each hedge fund index toward a variety of macroeconomic and financial variables and test whether these exposures have the ability to forecast expected hedge fund index returns.

5.1 PREDICTABILITY OF HEDGE FUND INDEX RETURNS BY MOMENTS OF THE RETURN DISTRIBUTION

The assumptions of the mean−variance analysis developed by Markowitz (1952) have been debated extensively. Mean−variance optimization can be justified under either of two assumptions. First, investors who have quadratic preferences would not be concerned about extreme losses. Alternatively, the mean and variance would completely describe the return distribution if the asset returns are jointly normally distributed. However, the empirical regularity that asset returns are typically skewed and leptokurtic has been widely documented. In other words, in reality, extreme events occur more frequently than predicted by the normal distribution. This opens up space for higher-order moments to be consequential for expected security returns.

The literature related to the relation between skewness and expected asset returns dates back to Arditti (1967). In a Taylor series expansion of the utility function around expected future wealth, the third moment of future wealth becomes a priced factor. For a risk-averse investor with nonincreasing absolute risk aversion, the relationship between this third moment that can be interpreted as a measure of skewness and expected asset returns has to be negative. In other words, risk-averse investors would be more (less) reluctant to take investments that offer a low probability of large losses (gains) and a high probability of small gains (losses). Therefore, investors prefer assets that add to the skewness of their portfolios, and they accept lower expected returns from investments with higher co-skewness. Rubinstein (1973) and Kraus and Litzenberger (1976) develop more elaborate general equilibrium models in which the representative investor adjusts his or her portfolio such that the expected return on a risky security is equal to the risk-free rate plus a premium that is equal to the weighted sum of the co-moments of the expected return of the security with the investor's future wealth. In these models, the marginal rate of substitution between expected return and skewness times a risky asset's marginal contribution to the skewness of the market portfolio becomes a component of the expected return of the asset. Arzac and Bawa (1977) model investors that neglect admissible risks of failure and become concerned about safety when the probability of failure exceeds a certain threshold, to theorize that the contribution of an asset to the skewness of the market portfolio should become a component of the asset's expected return. More recently, Harvey and Siddique (2000) construct a similar model that focuses on the conditional skewness rather than unconditional skewness. They also document a negative relationship between the expected returns of individual securities and the returns on a factor-mimicking portfolio based on co-skewness. The common theme of these studies is that co-skewness is a potentially important determinant of expected returns.

More recently, another strand of literature has emerged that examines the role of idiosyncratic skewness in explaining security returns. Barberis and Huang (2008) build on the cumulative prospect theory of Tversky and Kahneman (1992) to model investors who use a transformed probability weighting function and overweight the tails of a return distribution. According to this model, some investors find it beneficial to hold a large, undiversified position in skewed securities and accept a negative excess return on such assets. Brunnermeier et al. (2007) arrive at similar predictions based on a model of optimal expectations, which hinges on the idea that investors derive current felicity from expected future utility flows; thus they are happier if they overestimate the probabilities of the world in which their investments pay off well. In their general equilibrium, the portfolios have idiosyncratically skewed returns and the skewness preferences of investors have asset pricing effects. In summary, economic theories based on behavioral biases predict a negative relationship between idiosyncratic skewness and expected returns.

As far as the fourth moment is concerned, following Kimball (1993) and Pratt and Zeckhauser (1987), Dittmar (2002) extends the three-moment pricing model and finds preference for lower kurtosis. Investors are averse to kurtosis and prefer stocks with lower probability mass in the tails of the distribution to stocks with higher probability mass in the tails of the distribution. According to the model, assets that make portfolio returns more leptokurtic are less desirable and should command higher expected returns.

The issue of higher order moments is even more crucial for hedge funds. As noted in Chapter 4, studies such as Fung and Hsieh (2001), Mitchell and Pulvino (2001), and Agarwal and Naik (2004) show that the dynamic trading strategies implemented by hedge funds cause fund returns to deviate from normality and generate significant tail risk exposure. Also, Brown et al. (2013) have shown that this type of tail risk may not be diversifiable which suggests that the cross-sectional dispersion in skewness and kurtosis measures could be an important factor explaining hedge fund index returns.

In the empirical analysis of this section, we use a 36-month rolling window estimation period to generate monthly time-series measures of the moments of each hedge fund index distribution. In other words, for each hedge fund index and each month, we calculate the mean, standard deviation, skewness, and kurtosis of the return distribution during the previous 36 months. For this analysis, we focus on investable indices provided by Dow Jones Credit Suisse. Thus, we start with three years of monthly returns from October 2004 to September 2007 to estimate the sample mean, standard deviation, skewness, and kurtosis for each index in our sample. Then, in the second stage, starting from October 2007, we update these statistics on a monthly basis in a rolling window fashion. Finally, we run pooled panel data regressions of one-month ahead hedge fund index returns on the moments of the index distributions:

$$R_{i,t+1} = \omega_t + \lambda_t \cdot \text{Mean}_{i,t} + X_t + \varepsilon_{i,t+1}$$
$$R_{i,t+1} = \omega_t + \lambda_t \cdot \text{SD}_{i,t} + X_t + \varepsilon_{i,t+1}$$
$$R_{i,t+1} = \omega_t + \lambda_t \cdot \text{Skew}_{i,t} + X_t + \varepsilon_{i,t+1} \tag{5.1}$$
$$R_{i,t+1} = \omega_t + \lambda_t \cdot \text{Kurt}_{i,t} + X_t + \varepsilon_{i,t+1}$$

where $R_{i,t+1}$ is the excess return of fund i in month $t + 1$. ω_t and λ_t are, respectively, the monthly intercepts and slope coefficients from the pooled panel data regressions. The standard errors are clustered by month to control for the problem of contemporaneous cross-sectional correlation among error terms. X_t denotes the set of macroeconomic and financial variables we control for in the regression specifications. We control for these variables to check whether any plausible relation between the moments of the index return distributions and the expected hedge fund index returns is robust after the potential predictive power of macroeconomic fundamentals is taken into account. The list of the macroeconomic and financial controls is as follows and these variables will be reused when we investigate the relation between expected hedge fund index returns and factor exposures in the next section.

1. *SMB*: The size factor from Fama and French (1993). Six quarterly rebalanced benchmark portfolios are constructed using two independent sorts on market equity and the ratio of book equity to market equity. The size breakpoint is the median NYSE market equity. The book-to-market ratio breakpoints are the thirtieth and seventieth NYSE percentiles. SMB is the average return on three small portfolios minus the average return on three big portfolios. Obtained from Kenneth R. French's online data library.

2. *HML*: The book-to-market factor from Fama and French (1993). The same benchmark portfolios are used as for the size factor above. The portfolios in each size group with high book-to-market ratios are called the value portfolios. The portfolios in each size group with low book-to-market ratios are called the growth portfolios. HML is the average return on two value portfolios minus the average return on two growth portfolios. Obtained from Kenneth R. French's online data library.

3. *MOM*: The momentum factor from Carhart (1997). Six monthly rebalanced benchmark portfolios are constructed using two independent

sorts on market equity and the prior returns from 12 months earlier to 2 months earlier. The size breakpoint is the median NYSE market equity. The prior return breakpoints are the thirtieth and seventieth NYSE percentiles. MOM is the average return on two high prior return portfolios minus the average return on two low prior return portfolios. Obtained from Kenneth R. French's online data library.

4. *Term Premium*: The yield difference between 10-year and 3-month Treasury securities. Obtained from the Federal Reserve.

5. *Default Premium*: The yield difference between BAA-rated and AAA-rated corporate bonds. Obtained from the Federal Reserve.

6. *Dividend Yield*: Aggregate dividend yield computed using the CRSP value-weighted index return with and without dividends following Fama and French (1988).

7. *Bond Factor*: Bond trend-following factor measured as the return of a primitive trend-following strategy of a bond lookback straddle. Obtained from David Hsieh's online data library.

8. *Currency Factor*: Currency trend-following factor measured as the return of a primitive trend-following strategy of a currency lookback straddle. Obtained from David Hsieh's online data library.

9. *Commodity Factor*: Commodity trend-following factor measured as the return of a primitive trend-following strategy of a commodity lookback straddle. Obtained from David Hsieh's online data library.

10. *Short-Term Rate Factor*: Short-term interest rate trend-following factor measured as the return of a primitive trend-following strategy of a short-term interest rate lookback straddle. Obtained from David Hsieh's online data library.

11. *Stock Index Factor*: Stock index trend-following factor measured as the return of a primitive trend-following strategy of a stock index lookback straddle. Obtained from David Hsieh's online data library.

12. *Variance Risk Premium*: The difference between the risk-neutral and objective expectations of realized variance, where the risk-neutral expectation of variance is measured as the end-of-month VIX and the realized variance is the sum of squared 5-minute log returns of the S&P 500 index over the month. Obtained from Hao Zhou's online data library.

13. *VIX*: Implied volatility which measures the market's forecast of the volatility of the S&P 500 index. Obtained from the Chicago Board Options Exchange.

14. *Inflation Rate*: Monthly inflation rate based on the US consumer price index. Obtained from the Bureau of Labor Statistics.

15. *Industrial Production*: Monthly growth rate of industrial production. Obtained from the Bureau of Labor Statistics.
16. *Non-farm Payroll*: Monthly percentage change in US non-farm payrolls. Obtained from the Bureau of Labor Statistics.

The descriptive statistics for the monthly time series of all of the macroeconomic and financial variables are presented in Table 5.1.

Table 5.2 presents the results from regressions of one-month ahead hedge fund index returns on the mean returns from the past 36 months and the macroeconomic and financial control variables. In each table, we report the results from five distinct specifications. First, we run a univariate regression of one-month ahead hedge fund index returns on only the return moment under consideration. Second, we add three financial variables, namely SMB, HML, and MOM, among the explanatory variables. Third, we augment the specifications by including the term premium, default premium, and dividend yield as additional control variables. Fourth, we include the five trend-following hedge fund factors proposed by Fung and Hsieh (2001) in the specifications. Finally, we add macroeconomic controls such as the implied volatility of the market, the inflation rate, the change in industrial production ,and the change in non-farm payrolls.

Table 5.2 shows that there is a negative relation between the expected hedge fund index returns and the mean returns from the previous 36 months, which indicates a mean reversion for hedge fund indices. In the univariate specification, the coefficient of the mean is -1.043 with a t-statistic of -2.63. This coefficient remains significant as additional control variables are added to the specifications and the associated t-statistics vary between -2.30 and -2.06. We also find that none of the financial variables except SMB in the fourth and fifth specifications have any predictive power for hedge fund index returns. Likewise, the term premium, default premium, and dividend yield cannot predict future index returns. Among the hedge fund factors proposed by Fung and Hsieh (2001), only the short-term rate factor has predictive power for expected index returns. In the fifth specification, we observe that the coefficient of the short-term rate factor is equal to -0.025 with a t-statistic of -2.53. Finally, in the same specification, we witness a positive relation between the change in industrial production and expected hedge fund index returns. The coefficient of the change in industrial production is equal to 1.249 with a t-statistic of 7.56. The R^2 for the univariate regression is only 2.42%, but it progressively increases to 27.20% as more control variables are introduced.

Table 5.1 Descriptive Statistics for Macroeconomic Variables

	Mean	SD	Min	10%	25%	Median	75%	90%	Max	Skew	Kurt	Data Interval
SMB	0.256	2.310	− 4.270	− 2.730	− 1.210	− 0.040	1.650	3.740	5.890	0.314	2.625	200410–201208
HML	0.009	2.505	− 9.930	− 2.370	− 1.170	− 0.030	1.480	3.010	7.660	− 0.403	5.579	200410–201208
MOM	0.058	5.365	− 34.750	− 5.030	− 1.320	0.380	2.890	4.610	12.520	− 3.055	20.599	200410–201208
Term premium	1.784	1.264	− 0.520	− 0.120	0.670	2.000	2.850	3.380	3.690	− 0.282	1.853	200410–201208
Default premium	1.214	0.577	0.620	0.810	0.900	0.990	1.320	1.680	3.380	2.244	7.612	200410–201208
Dividend yield	2.025	0.436	1.569	1.684	1.764	1.876	2.087	2.766	3.684	2.045	6.741	200410–201208
Bond factor	− 3.874	13.999	− 25.400	− 17.380	− 13.300	− 6.900	1.050	14.800	43.430	1.407	5.078	200410–201208
Currency factor	0.288	19.407	− 25.700	− 19.400	− 13.095	− 4.420	8.045	24.200	69.200	1.346	4.917	200410–201208
Commodity factor	0.029	15.168	− 23.000	− 18.300	− 9.900	− 2.500	5.600	22.700	40.600	0.904	3.454	200410–201208
Short-term rate factor	4.751	37.312	− 34.640	− 22.170	− 13.445	− 4.750	11.200	25.600	221.900	3.628	18.654	200410–201208
Stock index factor	− 3.635	12.293	− 26.600	− 19.500	− 11.455	− 4.455	3.250	9.700	42.810	0.842	4.770	200410–201208
Variance risk premium	15.893	17.726	− 7.750	1.466	5.415	8.706	22.682	35.594	83.850	1.972	7.274	200410–201208
VIX	21.324	9.863	10.420	12.040	14.020	18.430	25.250	34.540	59.890	1.621	5.878	200410–201208
Inflation rate	0.205	0.387	− 1.794	− 0.088	0.043	0.248	0.407	0.577	1.377	− 1.471	10.432	200410–201208
Industrial production	0.050	0.860	− 4.125	− 0.858	− 0.181	0.175	0.565	0.944	1.568	− 1.902	8.794	200410–201208
Non-farm payroll	0.014	0.205	− 0.609	− 0.275	− 0.042	0.065	0.141	0.196	0.398	− 1.405	4.777	200410–201208
S&P 500 return	0.004	0.045	− 0.169	− 0.061	− 0.018	0.011	0.032	0.053	0.108	− 0.781	4.598	200410–201208
Risk-free rate	0.153	0.162	0.000	0.000	0.010	0.110	0.315	0.410	0.440	0.530	1.694	200410–201208

Table 5.2 Predictability of Hedge Fund Index Returns by Mean of Returns and Macroeconomic Factors

	[1]	[2]	[3]	[4]	[5]
Mean	− 1.0429	− 0.8735	− 0.8599	− 0.8657	− 0.8039
	(− 2.63)	(− 2.06)	(− 2.11)	(− 2.30)	(− 2.07)
SMB		− 0.0664	− 0.2703	− 0.2268	− 0.2095
		(− 0.47)	(− 0.19)	(− 1.96)	(− 1.95)
HML		− 0.0760	− 0.1810	0.0107	− 0.0149
		(− 0.44)	(− 0.90)	(0.10)	(− 0.17)
MOM		− 0.0661	− 0.1197	− 0.0245	− 0.0349
		(− 1.52)	(− 1.96)	(− 0.67)	(− 1.13)
Term premium			0.0815	− 0.2271	− 0.5121
			(0.23)	(− 0.81)	(− 1.89)
Default premium			− 1.5539	0.1623	1.2855
			(− 1.63)	(0.17)	(1.13)
Dividend yield			0.8575	− 0.1759	0.1279
			(0.64)	(− 0.15)	(0.09)
Bond factor				− 0.0206	− 0.0125
				(− 1.21)	(− 0.85)
Currency factor				− 0.0102	− 0.0251
				(− 0.47)	(− 1.40)
Commodity factor				− 0.0159	0.0035
				(− 0.78)	(0.21)
Short-term rate factor				− 0.0395	− 0.0252
				(− 2.62)	(− 2.53)
Stock index factor				0.0164	− 0.0001
				(0.66)	(− 0.00)
VIX					− 0.0600
					(− 1.30)
Inflation rate					− 0.2751
					(− 0.46)
Industrial production					1.2493
					(7.56)
Non-farm payroll					− 0.7860
					(− 0.40)
Constant	− 0.2080	− 0.2177	− 0.1507	0.9364	0.9553
	(− 0.65)	(− 0.62)	(− 0.08)	(0.56)	(0.61)
R-squared	2.42%	3.66%	6.09%	22.28%	27.20%

Table 5.3 presents the results from regressions of one-month ahead hedge fund index returns on the standard deviation of returns from the past 36 months and the macroeconomic and financial control variables. In the univariate specification, the coefficient of standard deviation is 0.443 with a t-statistic of 2.48. This coefficient remains significant as additional

Table 5.3 Predictability of Hedge Fund Index Returns by Standard Deviation of Returns and Macroeconomic Factors

	[1]	[2]	[3]	[4]	[5]
SD	0.4433 (2.48)	0.3884 (2.31)	0.2990 (1.93)	0.2664 (2.19)	0.2413 (2.04)
SMB		− 0.0658 (− 0.47)	− 0.0262 (− 0.19)	− 0.2272 (− 1.93)	− 0.2118 (− 1.94)
HML		− 0.0823 (− 0.51)	− 0.1769 (− 0.91)	0.0106 (0.10)	− 0.0189 (− 0.22)
MOM		− 0.0719 (− 1.84)	− 0.1208 (− 2.11)	− 0.0279 (− 0.74)	− 0.0382 (− 1.24)
Term premium			0.0781 (0.23)	− 0.1968 (− 0.71)	− 0.4800 (− 1.69)
Default premium			− 1.5210 (− 1.60)	0.1715 (0.17)	1.2884 (1.13)
Dividend yield			1.0164 (0.73)	0.0033 (0.00)	0.3220 (0.22)
Bond factor				− 0.0214 (− 1.24)	− 0.0128 (− 0.86)
Currency factor				− 0.0105 (− 0.48)	− 0.0252 (− 1.39)
Commodity factor				− 0.0153 (− 0.72)	0.0042 (0.24)
Short-term rate factor				− 0.0391 (− 2.65)	− 0.0248 (− 2.49)
Stock index factor				0.0156 (0.64)	0.0002 (0.01)
VIX					− 0.0651 (− 1.41)
Inflation rate					− 0.2935 (− 0.49)
Industrial production					1.2567 (7.72)
Non-farm payroll					− 0.9170 (− 0.45)
Constant	− 1.6708 (− 1.94)	− 1.5041 (− 1.84)	− 1.5221 (− 0.78)	− 0.4338 (− 0.26)	− 0.2221 (− 0.14)
R-squared	1.65%	3.82%	5.63%	21.66%	26.64%

control variables are added to the specifications and the associated t-statistics vary between 1.93 and 2.31. The interpretation of this result is that a greater volatility in hedge fund index returns is related to significantly higher one-month ahead expected returns. The inferences from Table 5.2 regarding the macroeconomic variables remain the same. The short-term rate factor and the change in industrial production are robust predictors of future hedge fund index returns. SMB is also significant in the fourth and fifth specifications. We also observe that the coefficient of MOM is significantly negative in the third specification with a t-statistic of -2.11; however, this result is not robust to the inclusion of additional controls. The R^2 for the univariate regression is only 1.65%, but it progressively increases to 26.64% as more control variables are introduced.

Table 5.4 presents the results from regressions of one-month ahead hedge fund index returns on the skewness of returns from the past 36 months and the macroeconomic and financial control variables, whereas the skewness is replaced with the kurtosis of returns from the past 36 months in Table 5.5. We find that neither the skewness nor the kurtosis of index returns have any predictive power for future hedge fund index returns. In Table 5.4, the t-statistics for skewness are between -0.03 and 0.48. In Table 5.5, the t-statistics for kurtosis are between -0.77 and -0.27. The R^2 for the univariate regressions in both tables are very close to zero. The results indicate that although hedge fund indices exhibit non-normal distributions with significant skewness and kurtosis, these higher-order moments do not explain the cross section of expected hedge fund index returns. The coefficients of the short-term rate factor and the change in industrial production retain their significant coefficients, whereas SMB is no longer significant in any of the specifications. The coefficient of MOM is again significantly negative in the second and third specifications of both tables; however, this significance disappears once the trend-following hedge fund factors and macroeconomic variables are added to the specifications.

We also estimate a specification in which we include all moments of hedge fund index return distributions simultaneously using the following regression equation:

$$R_{i,t+1} = \omega_t + \lambda_{1,t} \cdot \mathrm{Mean}_{i,t} + \lambda_{2,t} \cdot \mathrm{SD}_{i,t} + \lambda_{3,t} \cdot \mathrm{Skew}_{i,t} + \lambda_{4,t} \cdot \mathrm{Kurt}_{i,t}$$
$$+ X_t + \varepsilon_{i,t+1}$$

$$(5.2)$$

The results are presented in Table 5.6. The mean of the index returns from the past 36 months can still predict one-month ahead hedge fund index returns in all of the specifications. The coefficients vary between -1.436 and -1.217 with t-statistics between -3.00 and -2.63. An interesting result is that the standard deviation that has

Table 5.4 Predictability of Hedge Fund Index Returns by Skewness of Returns and Macroeconomic Factors

	[1]	[2]	[3]	[4]	[5]
Skewness	−0.0074 (−0.03)	0.0870 (0.28)	0.1414 (0.48)	0.0182 (0.07)	0.0070 (0.03)
SMB		−0.0567 (−0.39)	−0.0299 (−0.21)	−0.2215 (−1.83)	−0.2053 (−1.84)
HML		−0.1115 (−0.62)	−0.2100 (−1.05)	−0.0151 (−0.14)	−0.0383 (−0.46)
MOM		−0.0891 (−2.00)	−0.1357 (−2.28)	−0.0393 (−1.08)	−0.0489 (−1.59)
Term premium			0.4049 (1.10)	0.0635 (0.20)	−0.2687 (−0.91)
Default premium			−1.7228 (−1.79)	0.0108 (0.01)	1.1265 (0.98)
Dividend yield			1.2744 (0.95)	0.1839 (0.16)	0.6263 (0.43)
Bond factor				−0.0195 (−1.12)	−0.0120 (−0.79)
Currency factor				−0.0112 (−0.51)	−0.0268 (−1.46)
Commodity factor				−0.0118 (−0.58)	0.0075 (0.44)
Short-term rate factor				−0.0406 (−2.73)	−0.0256 (−2.56)
Stock index factor				0.0173 (0.67)	−0.0001 (−0.00)
VIX					−0.0636 (−1.37)
Inflation rate					−0.3599 (−0.57)
Industrial production					1.2606 (7.90)
Non-farm payroll					−0.5537 (−0.27)
Constant	−0.1856 (−0.48)	−0.0928 (−0.25)	−1.4803 (−0.80)	−0.3657 (−0.22)	−0.4084 (−0.26)
R-squared	0.00%	2.14%	5.08%	21.14%	26.23%

a positive relation with expected hedge fund index returns in Table 5.3 in all of the specifications is no longer significant. In Table 5.6, the t-statistics associated with the coefficient of standard deviation are between −0.80 and −0.08. In other words, the predictive power of standard deviation for future hedge fund index returns is subsumed by

Table 5.5 Predictability of Hedge Fund Index Returns by Kurtosis of Returns and Macroeconomic Factors

	[1]	[2]	[3]	[4]	[5]
Kurtosis	− 0.0210 (− 0.27)	− 0.0415 (− 0.52)	− 0.0559 (− 0.77)	− 0.0338 (− 0.56)	− 0.0324 (− 0.52)
SMB		− 0.0583 (− 0.41)	− 0.0325 (− 0.23)	− 0.2229 (− 1.83)	− 0.2059 (− 1.84)
HML		− 0.1140 (− 0.65)	− 0.2111 (− 1.06)	− 0.0185 (− 0.18)	− 0.0406 (− 0.49)
MOM		− 0.0902 (− 2.10)	− 0.1358 (− 2.31)	− 0.0405 (− 1.10)	− 0.0503 (− 1.64)
Term premium			0.4217 (1.20)	0.1055 (0.34)	− 0.2261 (− 0.79)
Default premium			− 1.7350 (− 1.80)	− 0.0032 (− 0.00)	1.1045 (0.95)
Dividend yield			1.3081 (0.97)	0.2418 (0.21)	0.6996 (0.48)
Bond factor				− 0.0193 (− 1.11)	− 0.1190 (− 0.79)
Currency factor				− 0.0114 (− 0.53)	− 0.0272 (− 1.47)
Commodity factor				− 0.0109 (− 0.53)	0.0085 (0.49)
Short-term rate factor				− 0.0406 (− 2.75)	− 0.0257 (− 2.56)
Stock index factor				0.0177 (0.69)	0.0000 (0.00)
VIX					− 0.0618 (− 1.31)
Inflation rate					− 0.3679 (− 0.58)
Industrial production					1.2578 (7.91)
Non-farm payroll					− 0.4776 (− 0.23)
Constant	− 0.0249 (− 0.05)	0.0870 (0.18)	− 1.3710 (− 0.71)	− 0.3663 (− 0.22)	− 0.4714 (− 0.30)
R-squared	0.05%	2.28%	5.27%	21.26%	26.33%

the predictive power of the mean of the index returns. Another curious finding is that, after controlling for the mean, the kurtosis has a significantly negative relation with expected hedge fund index returns in the fourth and fifth specifications, with t-statistics of − 2.24 and − 1.98, respectively. Our inferences regarding the macroeconomic variables are

Table 5.6 Predictability of Hedge Fund Index Returns by All Return Moments and Macroeconomic Factors

	[1]	[2]	[3]	[4]	[5]
Mean	− 1.4355 (− 2.87)	− 1.3203 (− 2.82)	− 1.4071 (− 3.00)	− 1.2918 (− 2.98)	− 1.2172 (− 2.63)
SD	0.2671 (1.29)	0.2556 (1.27)	0.1759 (1.05)	0.1459 (1.06)	0.1220 (0.93)
Skewness	− 0.0802 (− 0.21)	− 0.0294 (− 0.08)	− 0.1055 (− 0.26)	− 0.2565 (− 0.75)	− 0.2822 (− 0.80)
Kurtosis	− 0.1898 (− 1.73)	− 0.1828 (− 1.78)	− 0.1831 (− 1.71)	− 0.1811 (− 2.24)	− 0.1791 (− 1.98)
SMB		− 0.0865 (− 0.64)	− 0.0447 (− 0.33)	− 0.2386 (− 2.04)	− 0.2160 (− 2.01)
HML		− 0.0732 (− 0.44)	− 0.1589 (− 0.83)	0.0243 (0.23)	0.0040 (0.05)
MOM		− 0.0618 (− 1.45)	− 0.1067 (− 1.88)	− 0.0150 (− 0.38)	− 0.0265 (− 0.84)
Term premium			− 0.0438 (− 0.13)	− 0.3517 (− 1.25)	− 0.6202 (− 2.18)
Default premium			− 1.4138 (− 1.56)	0.2605 (0.25)	1.3608 (1.18)
Dividend yield			0.8592 (0.67)	− 0.2172 (− 0.18)	0.0282 (0.02)
Bond factor				− 0.0206 (− 1.21)	− 0.0132 (− 0.92)
Currency factor				− 0.0108 (− 0.49)	− 0.0259 (− 1.43)
Commodity factor				− 0.0165 (− 0.82)	0.0030 (0.17)
Short-term rate factor				− 0.0383 (− 2.59)	− 0.0244 (− 2.49)
Stock index factor				0.0164 (0.66)	− 0.0019 (− 0.10)
VIX					− 0.0485 (− 0.00)
Inflation rate					− 0.2400 (− 0.40)
Industrial production					1.2278 (7.23)
Non-farm payroll					− 0.5388 (− 0.26)
Constant	0.1327 (0.17)	0.1885 (0.26)	0.5533 (0.31)	1.6681 (0.97)	1.5285 (0.90)
R-squared	5.21%	6.46%	8.16%	23.71%	28.48%

the same, with the short-term rate factor and industrial production being significant predictors of future hedge fund index returns and SMB having a significantly negative coefficient in the fourth and fifth specifications.

To summarize the results from Tables 5.2 to 5.6, we find that the mean and the standard deviation of past index returns are significant predictors of one-month ahead hedge fund index returns; however, the predictive power of the mean subsumes that of the standard deviation when both moments are included in the regressions simultaneously. We do not observe any predictive power for skewness. The kurtosis has a negative relation with future hedge fund index returns, but only if all the other distributional moments and macroeconomic variables are controlled for. Cornish and Fisher (1937) argue that value at risk (VaR) is a function of the moments of a return distribution. For example, asset distributions with more left skewness and thicker tails have larger VaRs. Therefore, we calculate a VaR measure for each hedge fund index and each month using the methodology in Section 4.3, and test whether VaR predicts future hedge fund index returns using the following regression equation:

$$R_{i,t+1} = \omega_t + \lambda_t \cdot \text{VaR}_{i,t} + X_t + \varepsilon_{i,t+1} \qquad (5.3)$$

The results are presented in Table 5.7. We find that the VaR is a significant and robust predictor of one-month ahead hedge fund index returns. The coefficient of VaR in the univariate specification is equal to -0.098 with a t-statistic of -2.62. The t-statistics from the other four specifications range from -2.68 to -1.87. The significantly negative (positive) relation between the short-term rate factor (the change in industrial production) and the expected hedge fund index returns remains. Also, SMB and MOM still exhibit some predictive power for future hedge fund index returns in selected specifications.

5.2 PREDICTABILITY OF HEDGE FUND INDEX RETURNS BY EXPOSURES TO MACROECONOMIC RISK FACTORS

According to the intertemporal capital asset pricing model proposed by Merton (1973), variables that affect the investment opportunity sets of investors could be priced risk factors in equilibrium. Ross (1976) argues that financial securities that are affected by such risk factors should earn extra returns or risk premia in a risk-averse setting. Such

Table 5.7 Predictability of Hedge Fund Index Returns by VaR and Macroeconomic Factors					
	[1]	[2]	[3]	[4]	[5]
VaR	− 0.0981 (− 2.62)	− 0.0843 (− 2.25)	− 0.0649 (− 1.87)	− 0.0643 (− 2.68)	− 0.0607 (− 2.58)
SMB		− 0.0632 (− 0.45)	− 0.0245 (− 0.18)	− 0.2266 (− 1.95)	− 0.2113 (− 1.96)
HML		− 0.0820 (− 0.49)	− 0.1785 (− 0.89)	0.0129 (0.12)	− 0.0155 (− 0.18)
MOM		− 0.0708 (− 1.74)	− 0.1207 (− 2.01)	− 0.0262 (− 0.70)	− 0.0362 (− 1.17)
Term premium			0.0848 (0.25)	− 0.2207 (− 0.78)	− 0.5141 (− 1.86)
Default premium			− 1.5150 (− 1.59)	0.1949 (0.20)	1.3206 (1.17)
Dividend yield			0.9852 (0.72)	− 0.0420 (− 0.03)	0.2884 (0.20)
Bond factor				− 0.0213 (− 1.26)	− 0.0129 (− 0.88)
Currency factor				− 0.0104 (− 0.48)	− 0.0253 (− 1.41)
Commodity factor				− 0.0159 (− 0.77)	0.0035 (0.21)
Short-term rate factor				− 0.0390 (− 2.59)	− 0.0246 (− 2.49)
Stock index factor				0.1053 (0.62)	− 0.0004 (− 0.02)
VIX					− 0.0651 (− 1.43)
Inflation rate					− 0.2973 (− 0.49)
Industrial production					1.2595 (7.73)
Non-farm payroll					− 0.8734 (− 0.44)
Constant	− 1.2646 (− 1.95)	− 1.1309 (− 1.81)	− 1.1932 (− 0.62)	− 0.1207 (− 0.07)	0.0379 (0.02)
R-squared	2.30%	3.71%	5.58%	21.73%	26.74%

theoretical models have refrained from indicating which variables are likely to be globally priced risk factors. Macroeconomic variables are among the potential candidates because innovations in these variables can have systematic impact on corporations' cash flow generating abilities, discount factors, and investment opportunities. For example, if there is an unexpected increase in the announced inflation rate, this can lead investors to revise their expectations about future inflation rates upward. Consequently, nominal interest rates may increase, thereby depressing equity prices. Also, inflation surprises may trigger restrictive macroeconomic policies by governments, which can further pull equity prices downward through reduced expected corporate cash flows. Similarly, positive shocks to the industrial production growth or negative shocks to the unemployment rate may cause investors to revise their estimates regarding firms' future growth rates upward and have a positive impact on equity prices. These potential connections imply that the changes in macroeconomic fundamentals can affect the prices of financial securities. Hedge funds invest in a wide variety of instruments in the financial markets, and, as a result, their performances may also be influenced by the funds' sensitivities toward macroeconomic fundamentals.

The asset pricing literature has investigated the relationship between financial security prices and various macroeconomic and financial variables. Bodie (1976) and Fama (1981) are among the first studies that document a negative link between inflation and equity values. Chan et al. (1985), Chen et al. (1986), and Chen (1991) focus on macroeconomic variables such as inflation, term premium, default premium, and changes in aggregate production and find that these variables impact expected returns of financial securities. Moreover, studies such as Fama and Schwert (1987), Keim and Stambaugh (1986), Campbell and Shiller (1988), and Fama and French (1988, 1989) document that the dividend yield, term premium, default premium, and short-term interest rate can predict the expected returns of stocks and bonds. One drawback of these studies is that they often analyze the relationship between security values and the macroeconomic variables themselves. However, from a risk perspective, it is the exposure or the sensitivity of a security to the macroeconomic fundamentals that should determine the security's expected return. Also, until recently, no study had analyzed the relationship between hedge fund returns and macroeconomic fundamentals. Bali et al. (2011) fill both of these gaps in the literature by calculating hedge funds' exposures to various financial and macroeconomic risk factors through measures of factor sensitivities or factor betas and examining the ability of these factor betas to forecast the cross-sectional variation in hedge fund returns. In this section, we use the methodology in Bali et al. (2011) and apply it to hedge fund indices rather than individual hedge funds in a more recent sample which covers the 2008 credit crunch and the post-crisis period. Our goal is not inventing new factors that are able to explain hedge fund returns, but testing the significance of the aforementioned macroeconomic and financial risk factors' betas on predicting the cross-sectional variation in monthly returns of hedge fund indices.

We run a two-stage regression-based parametric test to assess the predictive power of factor betas over future hedge fund index returns. In the first stage, we estimate univariate factor betas for each hedge fund index from the univariate time-series regressions of hedge fund excess returns on a particular macroeconomic or financial variable over a 36-month rolling-window period. In the second stage, the cross section of one-month ahead hedge fund index excess returns is regressed on the univariate factor betas derived from the first stage. For this analysis, we focus on investable indices provided by Dow Jones Credit Suisse. Thus, we start with the three years of monthly returns from October 2004 to September 2007 to estimate the factor betas for each index in our sample, and then follow a monthly rolling regression approach with a fixed estimation window of 36 months to generate the time-series monthly factor betas based on the following regression equation:

$$R_{i,t} = \alpha_{i,t} + \beta_{i,t}^F F_t + \varepsilon_{i,t} \tag{5.4}$$

where $R_{i,t}$ is the excess return on hedge fund index i in month t and F_t is the macroeconomic or financial risk factor F in month t. $\alpha_{i,t}$ and $\beta_{i,t}^F$ are, respectively, the alpha and the risk factor F's beta for hedge fund index i in month t. The macroeconomic or financial risk factor F in the regression equation represents one of the 16 variables listed earlier. We also include the monthly return of the S&P 500 index and the risk-free rate among the universe of potential factors. Equation (5.4) is not one single regression, but it is a set of 18 regression equations in which each regression equation is run for each macroeconomic and financial risk factor separately.

In the second stage, starting from October 2007, we use the Fama–Macbeth (1973) cross-sectional regressions of one-month ahead hedge fund index excess returns on the factor betas:

$$R_{i,t+1} = \delta_t + \lambda_t \beta_{i,t}^F + \varepsilon_{i,t+1} \tag{5.5}$$

where $R_{i,t+1}$ is the excess return on hedge fund index i in month $t+1$ and $\beta_{i,t}^{F}$ is the risk factor F's beta for hedge fund index i in month t estimated using Eq. (5.4). δ_t and λ_t are, respectively, the monthly intercepts and slope coefficients from the Fama—Macbeth regressions. Equation (5.5) is also not one single regression, but it is a set of 18 regression equations in which each regression equation is run for each macroeconomic and financial risk factor separately.

Table 5.8 presents the time-series average slope coefficients or the average of λ_t's from Eq. (5.5), using as the independent variable the univariate factor betas that are estimated using a fixed 36-month rolling-window period. The corresponding Newey and West (1987) t-statistics are reported in parentheses. It is worthwhile to emphasize once again that each slope coefficient and t-statistic in Table 5.8 comes from a different univariate regression, and the results should not be interpreted as the outcome of a single multivariate regression.

Among the three factors that are often used to explain the cross section of equity returns, only the momentum beta seems to be significantly related to one-month ahead hedge fund index returns. The coefficient of the momentum beta is -3.63 with a t-statistic of -2.31. We do not find any relation between the betas for the term premium, default premium, and dividend yield factors and expected hedge fund index returns. There is also no significant link between one-month ahead index returns and the betas for the five trend-following factors of Fung and Hsieh (2001). The t-statistics for the coefficients of these five factor betas are between -0.78 and 1.14. Although the exposure of hedge fund index returns toward the market implied volatility cannot predict one-month ahead index returns, we do find a significantly negative relationship between the variance risk premium beta and the future returns of hedge fund indices. The coefficient of the variance risk premium beta is equal to -12.93 with a t-statistic of -2.31. The exposures toward macroeconomic variables such as the inflation rate, the change in industrial production, and the change in non-farm payrolls cannot explain the cross section of expected hedge fund index returns. Finally, although the market beta has an insignificant coefficient, there is a significantly negative relation between the risk-free rate beta and one-period ahead hedge fund index returns. The coefficient of

Table 5.8 Univariate Regressions of 1-Month Ahead Hedge Fund Index Returns on Factor Betas	
SMB	0.1890 (0.21)
HML	1.0546 (1.12)
MOM	−3.6251 (−2.31)
Term premium	−0.4893 (−0.71)
Default premium	−0.8076 (−1.23)
Dividend yield	−1.3154 (−1.21)
Bond factor	7.0441 (1.11)
Currency factor	11.6394 (1.14)
Commodity factor	−3.7671 (−0.78)
Short-term rate factor	17.1865 (0.92)
Stock index factor	4.1162 (0.70)
Variance risk premia	−12.9319 (−2.31)
VIX	−9.9003 (−1.06)
Inflation rate	−0.0324 (−0.22)
Industrial production	−0.1022 (−0.15)
Non-farm payroll	0.0134 (0.26)
S&P 500 return	1.3603 (0.98)
Risk-free rate	−0.3897 (−2.33)

the risk-free rate beta is equal to −0.39 with a t-statistic of −2.33. To summarize all these results, we find that hedge fund indices that are more exposed to the momentum, variance risk premium, and risk-free rate factors have significantly lower expected returns.

REFERENCES

Ackermann, C., McEnally, R., Ravenscraft, D., 1999. The performance of hedge funds: risk, return and incentives. J. Financ. 54, 833–874.

Agarwal, V., Naik, N.Y., 2004. Risks and portfolio decisions involving hedge funds. Rev. Financ. Stud. 17, 63–98.

Agarwal, V., Boyson, N.M., Naik, N.Y., 2009a. Hedge funds for retail investors? An examination of hedged mutual funds. J. Financ. Quant. Anal. 44, 273–305.

Agarwal, V., Daniel, N.D., Naik, N.Y., 2009b. Role of managerial incentives and discretion in hedge fund performance. J. Financ. 64, 2221–2256.

Agarwal, V., Daniel, N.D., Naik, N.Y., 2011. Do hedge funds manage their reported returns? Rev. Financ. Stud. 24, 3281–3320.

Agarwal, V., Jiang, W., Tang, Y., Yang, B., 2013. Uncovering hedge fund skill from the portfolio holdings they hide. J. Financ. 68, 739–783.

Aggarwal, R.K., Jorion, P., 2010. The performance of emerging hedge funds and managers. J. Financ. Econ. 96, 238–256.

Aiken, A.L., Clifford, C.P., Ellis, J., 2013. Out of the dark: hedge fund reporting biases and commercial databases. Rev. Financ. Stud. 26, 208–243.

Amin, G.S., Kat, H.M., 2003. Hedge fund performance 1990–2000: do the money machines really add value? J. Financ. Quant. Anal. 38, 251–274.

Aragon, G.O., 2007. Share restrictions and asset pricing: evidence from the hedge fund industry. J. Financ. Econ. 83, 33–58.

Aragon, G.O., Martin, J.S., 2012. A unique view of hedge fund derivatives usage: safeguard or speculation. J. Financ. Econ. 105, 436–456.

Aragon, G.O., Nanda, V., 2012. Tournament behavior in hedge funds: high-water marks, fund liquidation and managerial stake. Rev. Financ. Stud. 25, 937–974.

Arditti, F.D., 1967. Risk and the required return on equity. J. Financ. 22, 19–36.

Arzac, E.R., Bawa, V.S., 1977. Portfolio choice and equilibrium in capital markets with safety-first investors. J. Financ. Econ. 4, 277–288.

Bali, T.G., 2003. An extreme value approach to estimating volatility and value at risk. J. Bus. 76, 83–108.

Bali, T.G., 2007. A generalized extreme value approach to financial risk measurement. J. Money Credit Bank. 39, 1611–1647.

Bali, T.G., Theodossiou, P., 2007. A conditional SGT VAR approach with alternative GARCH models. Ann. Oper. Res. 151, 241–267

Bali, T.G., Theodossiou, P., 2008. Risk measurement performance of alternative distribution functions. J. Risk Insur. 75, 411–437.

Bali, T.G., Weinbaum, D., 2007. A conditional extreme value volatility estimator based on high-frequency returns. J. Econ. Dyn. Control 31, 361–397.

Bali, T.G., Gokcan, S., Liang, B., 2007. Value at risk and the cross-section of hedge fund returns. J. Bank. Financ. 31, 1135–1166.

Bali, T.G., Demirtas, K.O., Levy, H., 2009. Is there an intertemporal relation between downside risk and expected returns? J. Financ. Quant. Anal. 44, 883–909.

Bali, T.G., Brown, S.J., Caglayan, M.O., 2011. Do hedge funds' exposures to risk factors predict their future returns? J. Financ. Econ. 101, 36–68.

Bali, T.G., Brown, S.J., Caglayan, M.O., 2012. Systematic risk and the cross-section of hedge fund returns. J. Financ. Econ. 106, 114–131.

Bali, T.G., Brown, S., Demirtas, K.O., 2013. Do hedge funds outperform stocks and bonds?. Manage. Sci. (forthcoming).

Barberis, N., Huang, M., 2008. Stocks as lotteries: the implications of probability weighting for security prices. Am. Econ. Rev. 98, 2066–2100.

Ben-David, I., Franzoni, F., Moussawi, R., 2012. Hedge fund stock trading in the financial crisis of 2007–2009. Rev. Financ. Stud. 25, 1–54.

Berkowitz, J., 2001. Testing density forecasts with applications to risk management. J. Bus. Econ. Stat. 19, 465–474.

Berkowitz, J., O'Brian, J., 2002. How accurate are value-at-risk models at commercial banks. J. Financ. 57, 1093–1111.

Black, F., Scholes, M., 1973. The pricing of options and corporate liabilities. J. Polit. Econ. 81, 637–654.

Bodie, Z., 1976. Common stocks as hedge against inflation. J. Financ. 31, 459–470.

Bollen, N.P., Pool, V.K., 2008. Conditional return smoothing in the hedge fund industry. J. Financ. Quant. Anal. 43, 267–296.

Bollen, N.P., Pool, V.K., 2009. Do hedge fund managers misreport returns? Evidence from the pooled distribution. J. Financ. 64, 2257–2288.

Bollen, N.P., Pool, V.K., 2012. Suspicious patterns in hedge fund returns and the risk of fraud. Rev. Financ. Stud. 25, 2673–2702.

Boyson, N.M., Stahel, C.W., Stulz, R.M., 2010. Hedge fund contagion and liquidity shocks. J. Financ. 65, 1789–1816.

Brav, A., Jiang, W., Partnoy, F., Thomas, R., 2008. Hedge fund activism, corporate governance and firm performance. J. Financ. 63, 1729–1775.

Brophy, D.J., Ouimet, P.P., Sialm, C., 2009. Hedge funds as investors of last resort? Rev. Financ. Stud. 22, 541–574.

Brown, S.J., Goetzmann, W., Liang, B., Schwarz, C., 2008. Mandatory disclosure and operational risk: evidence from hedge fund registration. J. Financ. 63, 2785–2816.

Brown, S.J., Goetzmann, W., Ibbotson, R.G., Ross, S.A., 1992. Survivorship bias in performance studies. Rev. Financ. Stud. 5, 553–580.

Brown, S.J., Goetzmann, W., Park, J., 2001. Careers and survival: competition and risk in the hedge fund and CTA industry. J. Financ. 56, 1869–1886.

Brown, S.J., Grundy, B.D., Lewis, C.M., Vermijmeren, P., 2012. Convertibles and hedge funds as distributors of equity exposure. Rev. Financ. Stud. 25, 3077–3112.

Brown, S.J., Gregoriou, G., Pascalau, R., 2013. Is it possible to overdiversify? The case of hedge funds. Rev. Asset Pricing Stud. 2, 89–110.

Brunnermeier, M.K., Nagel, S., 2004. Hedge funds and the technology bubble. J. Financ. 59, 2013–2040.

Brunnermeier, M.K., Gollier, C., Parker, J.A., 2007. Optimal beliefs, asset prices and the preference for skewed returns. Am. Econ. Rev. 97, 159–165.

Campbell, J.Y., Shiller, R., 1988. The dividend-price ratio and expectations of future dividends and discount factors. Rev. Financ. Stud. 1, 195–228.

Carhart, M.M., 1997. On persistence in mutual fund performance. J. Financ. 52, 57–82.

Cassar, G., Gerakos, J., 2011. Hedge funds: pricing controls and the smoothing of self-reported returns. Rev. Financ. Stud. 24, 1698–1734.

Chan, K.C., Chen, N.F., Hsieh, D.A., 1985. An exploratory investigation of the firm size effect. J. Financ. Econ. 14, 451–471.

Chen, L.W., Chen, F., 2009. Does concurrent management of mutual and hedge funds create conflicts of interest? J. Bank. Financ. 33, 1423–1433.

Chen, N.F., 1991. Financial investment opportunities and the macroeconomy. J. Financ. 46, 529–554.

Chen, N.F., Roll, R., Ross, S.A., 1986. Economic forces and the stock market. J. Bus. 59, 383–403.

Chen, Y., 2011. Derivatives use and risk taking: evidence from the hedge fund industry. J. Financ. Quant. Anal. 46, 1073–1106.

Chen, Y., Liang, B., 2007. Do market timing hedge funds time the market? J. Financ. Quant. Anal. 42, 827–856.

Coggan, P., 2008. Guide to Hedge Funds. Profile Books, London, UK.

Cornish, E.A., Fisher, R.A., 1937. Moments and cumulants in the specification of distributions. Extrait de la Revue de l'Institute International de Statistique 4, 1–14 (Reprinted in Fisher, R.A., 1950. Contributions to Mathematical Statistics, Wiley, New York).

Darolles, S., Vaissie, M., 2012. The alpha and omega of fund of hedge fund added value. J. Bank. Financ. 36, 1067–1078.

Deuskar, P., Pollet, J.M., Wang, Z.J., Zheng, L., 2011. The good or the bad? Which mutual fund managers join hedge funds. Rev. Financ. Stud. 24, 3008–3024.

Dichev, I., Yu, G., 2011. Higher risk, lower returns: what hedge fund investors really earn. J. Financ. Econ. 100, 248–263.

Ding, B., Shawky, H.A., Tian, J., 2009. Liquidity shocks, size and the relative performance of hedge fund strategies. J. Bank. Financ. 33, 883–891.

Dittmar, R.F., 2002. Nonlinear pricing kernels, kurtosis preference and evidence from the cross section of equity returns. J. Financ. 57, 369–403.

Eling, M., Faust, R., 2010. The performance of hedge funds and mutual funds in emerging markets. J. Bank. Financ. 34, 1993–2009.

Eling, M., Schuhmacher, F., 2007. Does the choice of performance measure influence the evaluation of hedge funds? J. Bank. Financ. 31, 2632–2647.

Fama, E.F., 1981. Stock returns, real activity, inflation and money. Am. Econ. Rev. 71, 545–565.

Fama, E.F., French, K.R., 1988. Dividend yields and expected stock returns. J. Financ. Econ. 22, 3–25.

Fama, E.F., French, K.R., 1989. Business conditions and expected returns on stocks and bonds. J. Financ. Econ. 25, 23–49.

Fama, E.F., French, K.R., 1993. Common risk factors in the returns on stocks and bonds. J. Financ. Econ. 33, 3–56.

Fama, E.F., Macbeth, J.D., 1973. Risk and return: some empirical tests. J. Polit. Econ. 81, 607–636.

Fama, E.F., Schwert, G.W., 1977. Asset returns and inflation. J. Financ. Econ. 5, 115–146.

Fung, W., Hsieh, D.A., 1997. Empirical characteristics of dynamic trading strategies: the case of hedge funds. Rev. Financ. Stud. 2, 275–302.

Fung, W., Hsieh, D.A., 2000. Performance characteristics of hedge funds and commodity funds: natural vs. spurious biases. J. Financ. Quant. Anal. 35, 291–307.

Fung, W., Hsieh, D.A., 2001. The risk in hedge fund strategies: theory and evidence from trend followers. Rev. Financ. Stud. 14, 313–341.

Fung, W., Hsieh, D.A., Naik, N.Y., Ramadorai, T., 2008. Hedge funds: performance, risk and capital formation. J. Financ. 63, 1777–1803.

Griffin, J.M., Xu, J., 2009. How smart are the smart guys? A unique view from hedge fund stock holdings. Rev. Financ. Stud. 22, 2531–2570.

Grinblatt, M., Titman, S., 1989. Mutual fund performance: an analysis of quarterly portfolio holdings. J. Bus. 62, 393–416.

Hansen, B.E., 1994. Autoregressive conditional density estimation. Int. Econ. Rev. 35, 705–730.

Harvey, C.R., Siddique, A., 2000. Conditional skewness in asset pricing tests. J. Financ. 55, 1263–1295.

Hodder, J.E., Jackwerth, J.C., 2007. Incentive contracts and hedge fund management. J. Financ. Quant. Anal. 42, 811–826.

Ingersoll, J.E., 1977. A contingent-claims valuation of convertible securities. J. Financ. 32, 289–321.

Jagannathan, R., Malakhov, A., Novikov, D., 2010. Do hot hands exist among hedge fund managers? An empirical evaluation. J. Financ. 65, 217–255.

Jiang, W., Li, K., Wang, W., 2012. Hedge funds and chapter 11. J. Financ. 67, 513–559.

Keim, D.B., Stambaugh, E.F., 1986. Predicting returns in the stock and bond markets. J. Financ. Econ. 17, 357–390.

Kimball, M., 1993. Standard risk aversion. Econometrica 61, 589–611.

Klein, A., Zur, E., 2009. Entrepreneurial shareholder activism: hedge funds and other private investors. J. Financ. 64, 187–229.

Klein, A., Zur, E., 2011. The impact of hedge fund activism on the target firm's existing bondholders. Rev. Financ. Stud. 24, 1735–1771.

Kosowski, R., Naik, N.Y., Teo, M., 2007. Do hedge funds deliver alpha? A Bayesian and bootstrap analysis. J. Financ. Econ. 84, 229–264.

Kouwenberg, R., Ziemba, W.T., 2007. Incentives and risk taking in hedge funds. J. Bank. Financ. 31, 3291–3310.

Kraus, A., Litzenberger, R.H., 1976. Skewness preference and the valuation of risk assets. J. Financ. 31, 1085–1100.

L'Habitant, F., 2006. Handbook of Hedge Funds. John Wiley and Sons, Chichester, UK.

Li, H., Zhang, X., Zhao, R., 2011. Investing in talents: manager characteristics and hedge fund performances. J. Financ. Quant. Anal. 46, 59–82.

Liang, B., 2000. Hedge funds: the living and the dead. J. Financ. Quant. Anal. 35, 309–326.

Liang, B., Park, H., 2010. Predicting hedge fund failure: a comparison of risk measures. J. Financ. Quant. Anal. 45, 199–222.

Liu, X., Mello, A.S., 2011. The fragile capital structure of hedge funds and limits to arbitrage. J. Financ. Econ. 102, 491–506.

Markowitz, H., 1952. Portfolio selection. J. Financ. 7, 77−91.

Massoud, N., Nandy, D., Saunders, A., Song, K., 2011. Do hedge funds trade on private information? Evidence from syndicated lending and short-selling. J. Financ. Econ. 99, 477−499.

McNeil, A.J., Frey, R., 2000. Estimation of tail-related risk measures for heteroscedastic financial time series: an extreme value approach. J. Empir. Financ. 7, 271−300.

Merton, R.C., 1973. An intertemporal asset pricing model. Econometrica 41, 867−887.

Mitchell, M., Pulvino, T., 2001. Characteristics of risk and return in risk arbitrage. J. Financ. 56, 2135−2175.

Newey, W.K., West, K.D., 1987. A simple, positive semi-definite, heteroskedasticity and autocorrelation consistent covariance matrix. Econometrica 55, 703−708.

Nohel, T., Wang, Z.J., Zheng, L., 2010. Side-by-side management of hedge funds and mutual funds. Rev. Financ. Stud. 23, 2342−2373.

Patton, A.J., 2009. Are market neutral hedge funds really market neutral? Rev. Financ. Stud. 22, 2495−2530.

Pratt, J., Zeckhauser, R., 1987. Proper risk aversion. Econometrica 55, 143−154.

Ramadorai, T., 2012. The secondary market for hedge funds and the closed hedge fund premium. J. Financ. 67, 479−512.

Ross, S.A., 1976. The arbitrage theory of capital asset pricing. J. Econ. Theory 13, 341−360.

Rubinstein, M., 1973. The fundamental theory of parameter-preference security valuation. J. Financ. Quant. Anal. 8, 61−69.

Sadka, R., 2010. Liquidity risk and the cross-section of hedge fund returns. J. Financ. Econ. 98, 54−71.

Schaub, N., Schmid, M., 2013. Hedge fund liquidity and performance: evidence from the financial crisis. J. Bank. Financ. 37, 671−692.

Stefanini, F., 2006. Investment Strategies of Hedge Funds. John Wiley and Sons, Chichester, UK.

Sun, Z., Wang, A., Zheng, L., 2012. The road less traveled: strategy distinctiveness and hedge fund performance. Rev. Financ. Stud. 25, 96−143.

Teo, M., 2009. The geography of hedge funds. Rev. Financ. Stud. 22, 3531−3561.

Teo, M., 2011. The liquidity risk of liquid hedge funds. J. Financ. Econ. 100, 24−44.

Tversky, A., Kahneman, D., 1992. Advances in prospect theory: cumulative representation of uncertainty. J. Risk Uncertainty 5, 297−323.

Printed and bound by CPI Group (UK) Ltd, Croydon, CR0 4YY

08/05/2025

01864771-0003